HUNGARIAN UPRISING

BUDAPEST'S CATACLYSMIC TWELVE DAYS
1956

LOUIS ARCHARD

Pen & Sword
MILITARY

First published in Great Britain in 2018 by
PEN AND SWORD MILITARY
an imprint of
Pen and Sword Books Ltd
47 Church Street
Barnsley
South Yorkshire S70 2AS

ISBN 978 1 52670 802 1

Typeset by Aura Technology and Software Services, India
Maps by George Anderson
Printed and bound by CPI Group (UK) Ltd, Croydon, CR0 4YY

Pen & Sword Books Ltd incorporates the imprints of Pen & Sword
Archaeology, Atlas, Aviation, Battleground, Discovery, Family History, History, Maritime,
Military, Naval, Politics, Railways, Select, Social History, Transport, True Crime, Claymore Press,
Frontline Books, Leo Cooper, Praetorian Press, Remember When, Seaforth Publishing and Wharncliffe.

For a complete list of Pen and Sword titles please contact
Pen and Sword Books Limited
47 Church Street, Barnsley, South Yorkshire, S70 2AS, England
email: enquiries@pen-and-sword.co.uk
website: www.pen-and-sword.co.uk

CONTENTS

An altered road sign warns of tanks in Budapest's Szentkirályi Street.
(Fortepan: Pesti Srác)

Talpra Magyar, hí a haza!
Itt az idő, most vagy soha!
Rabok legyünk vagy szabadok?

On your feet, Magyar, the homeland calls!
The time is here, now or never!
Shall we be slaves or free?

Sándor Petdwwőfi, *National Song*

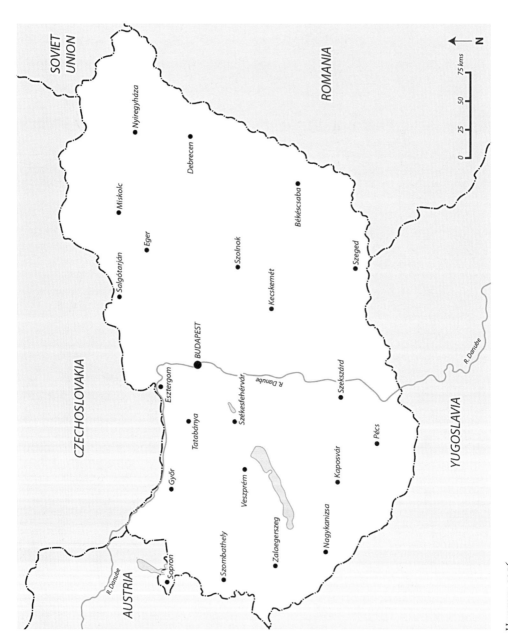

Hungary, 1956.

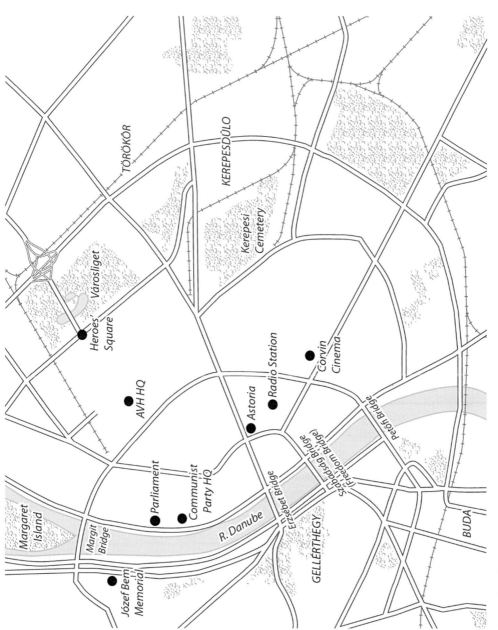

Central Budapest, 1956.

CHRONOLOGY

1948

June: Communists under Mátyás Rákosi take total control in Hungary

1949

15 October: execution of László Rajk

1953

4 July: Imre Nagy announces his 'New Course'

1956

25 February: Nikita Khrushchev makes his 'Secret Speech'

13 July: Mikoyan deposes Rákosi; Ernő Gerő takes his place

6 October: reburial of Rajk

22 October: students demonstrate in support of Gomułka in Poland

23 October: violence erupts as large-scale demonstrations become anti-Soviet; Gerő requests Soviet troops to stop violence

24 October: Imre Nagy becomes prime minister

28 October: after fierce fighting with Hungarian insurgents, the Soviets agree to a ceasefire

31 October: Khrushchev confirms that Soviets will use force to end the uprising

3 November: János Kádár appointed Nagy's successor as prime minister

4 November: Soviet troops attack insurgents

11 November: last resistance to Soviet forces in Hungary ends

1958

16 June: execution of Imre Nagy

1989

16 June: Imre Nagy is reburied in Budapest

AUTHOR'S NOTE

I visited Budapest in the autumn of 2007 – nearly ten years ago at the time of writing – and was very taken with it. I enjoyed the coffees and elaborate cakes served in the city's elegant coffee houses, appreciated as a novelty riding in the city's subway cars (because I was told that they had come second-hand from the Moscow Metro) and the beauty of the earliest part of the network (Budapest has the second oldest underground railway system in the world, after London) and generally soaked up the historic atmosphere. But I also noticed that many of the buildings in the city centre were still pockmarked with bullet holes and other damage and I soon guessed that this must be a relic of the 1956 uprising against the Soviets that had been focused in the Hungarian capital.

The Hungarian Uprising was a key point during the Cold War, one of those moments when the Cold War became hot. Khrushchev's decision to use military force to suppress the uprising once and for all demonstrated Soviet determination to preserve the sphere of influence that the USSR had established in Eastern Europe in the years immediately following the Second World War. That Soviet determination is what would turn the uprising into a tragedy, although it is difficult not to feel the exhilaration of the insurgents as at first they succeed beyond their wildest dreams. President Eisenhower's decision not to intervene in Hungary demonstrated that the Western powers were not willing to risk an open conflict with the Soviet Union, despite American rhetoric about rolling back communism and liberating the peoples of Eastern Europe.

But there is so much more to the story of the Hungarian Uprising than the superpower politics, fascinating though that can be. This was an organic revolution, driven by a sense that people had simply had enough. Looking at the account of the protests in Budapest on 23 October 1956, and at the student mass meeting the night before that had arranged it, it is striking that decisions that would later turn out to be crucial seem to have been taken as a result of interventions by people whose names went unrecorded. The Sixteen Points, the manifesto of the uprising, was drafted effectively by committee, a committee whose names have also gone unrecorded.

Although leaders did later emerge, no one of them was able to dominate the others. Even Imre Nagy, whose name is perhaps the most famous of the 1956

Flags hanging in Budapest's Mátyás Street. (Fortepan: Fortepan)

revolutionaries, often seems to have been scrambling to catch up with what was happening on the streets and struggled at first to understand the nature of what he was trying to lead. It's easy to feel sympathy for Imre Nagy, clearly a decent man trying to do his best under very difficult circumstances. However, although the uprising is the not the most controversial subject in Hungarian history (an honour that goes to the Treaty of Trianon, the settlement between the Allies and what had been the Hapsburg Empire at the end of the First World War), it is still a sensitive and controversial subject in Hungary itself and there are many interpretations of Imre Nagy and the decisions that he took.

The convention for names in Hungarian is to give the family name first, followed by the given name, so in Hungarian the prime minister would be known as Nagy Imre. However, in order to avoid confusion, I have given Hungarian names in the order which is familiar to English speakers.

The Hungarian Communist Party changed name twice in the period under discussion in this book, becoming the Hungarian Working People's Party and then the Hungarian Socialist Workers' Party. For the sake of avoiding further confusion, I have referred to it as the Hungarian Communist Party throughout.

I am grateful to Emese Bogya for her help with translations from Hungarian. I'd also like to thank my editor at Pen & Sword for all his support and advice. Finally, I'd like to thank Katie for all of her support. This one's for you.'

1. HUNGARY BECOMES A PEOPLE'S DEMOCRACY, 1944–53

In late 1944 and 1945, as the Allies advanced and the forces of Nazi Germany were pushed back, there was a feeling of rebirth and beginning again across Europe. In German, they called it *Stunde null* – Zero hour, the moment at which the fighting passed on, silence fell and the war was finally over – but the feeling was common across the continent.

Many Hungarians had believed that their country would be liberated by British or American forces advancing from the West as it was too geopolitically significant to leave to the Russians. However, despite this belief it would be the Red Army that pushed Nazi Germany out of Hungary from autumn 1944 onwards. On 29 October 1944, troops of the 2nd Ukrainian Front, commanded by General Malinovsky, began their offensive against Budapest itself. Soviet and Romanian troops entered the city's eastern suburbs on 7 November and when, on 26 December, the last road linking Budapest with Vienna was cut, the Hungarian capital was surrounded. Hitler had declared Budapest to be a fortress city, to be defended to the last man. The siege would last for fifty-one days.

Before the Second World War, Hungary had been ruled by Miklós Horthy. Horthy was a former admiral in the Austro-Hungarian Navy who had come to power in the period of instability that followed the defeat of the Habsburg Empire in the First World War, restoring order after the establishment of the Hungarian Soviet Republic under Béla Kun and its subsequent defeat by a Romanian army.

Although Horthy initially banned both the Hungarian Communist Party and the fascist Arrow Cross, Hungary became increasingly closely aligned with Nazi Germany for economic reasons, as a protection against Soviet communism and because Hitler tore up the settlements that had been put into place in eastern and central Europe as a result of the peace treaties that ended the First World War. Having been part of the Habsburg Empire, one of the Central Powers along with Germany and the Ottoman Empire, and seen as one of the aggressors that had started the war, territory that had belonged to the pre-war Kingdom of Hungary was given to some of the new nation states that emerged from the ruins of the

Austro-Hungarian Empire. Transylvania, for example, had previously been part of Hungary but after the war representatives of its ethnic Romanian majority declared union with Romania and this was confirmed in the Treaty of Trianon between the victorious Allied powers and what had been Austria-Hungary. A desire to regain the territories lost at Trianon was an important part of Hungarian life between the First and Second World Wars.

Hungarian troops joined the Axis war effort formally in June 1941, sending troops and resources to help in Operation Barbarossa and declaring war on the Soviet Union on 27 June, five days after the German invasion began. Enthusiasm for the war in Hungary, however, was never high and suffered a serious blow

Admiral Miklós Horthy in 1921. Horthy came to power during the instability that gripped Hungary following the end of the First World War and ruled until he was deposed on Hitler's orders in October 1944. (Library of Congress)

when the Second Hungarian Army was nearly obliterated by the Soviets in January 1943 as part of the fighting around Stalingrad, at a cost of nearly 80,000 Hungarian dead.

By 1944, as an eventual Allied victory was looking increasingly likely, the Horthy government began to approach the Allies about a separate peace settlement, hoping to save the country from Soviet invasion and occupation. Hitler, furious at this betrayal, ordered German troops to invade and occupy Hungary on 19 March. Horthy was allowed to remain in place as Hungary's leader but the Hungarian government was effectively under German control. As the military situation continued to deteriorate, Horthy made another attempt to negotiate a separate peace in September; this came to German attention and this time the Germans seized Horthy's son as a hostage and on 15 October, as the Soviets were preparing their offensive against Budapest, forced the Admiral to abdicate in favour of the Arrow Cross leader, Ferenc Szálas. The Arrow Cross was a Hungarian political movement similar in ways to the Nazi Party in Germany (both were anti-Semitic and both believed in the idea of 'master races'), although there were differences and disagreements between the two as well.

By the time the Germans had replaced Horthy with Szálas, however, Hungary's post-war fate had already been determined. Churchill had gone to Moscow for discussions with Stalin. On 9 October, the two men met and agreed the so-called Percentages Deal, which allocated proportions of post-war influence in various countries between Britain and the Soviet Union. In this meeting Churchill effectively traded Soviet dominance in Eastern Europe for British dominance in Greece, then in the throes of its civil war between communist guerrillas and the British-backed government. Influence in Hungary would be split equally between Britain and the Soviet Union, 50/50. The two leaders sketched out their arrangement on a piece of paper and when they were done Churchill said to Stalin, 'Might it not be thought rather cynical if it seemed we had disposed of these issues, so fateful to millions of people, in such an offhand manner? Let us burn the paper?' Stalin, less troubled by qualms, responded, 'No, you keep it.'

The next day, British foreign secretary Anthony Eden met with the Soviet foreign minister, Vyacheslav Molotov. Molotov informed Eden that 'Marshal Stalin thought that after learning of the considerable losses sustained by the Red Army in Hungary, the army would not understand it if a principle of 50/50 were allotted.' He went on to inform Eden that 'the 75/25 principle was what the Soviet

Government proposed, for the reason that Hungary bordered on the Soviet Union and the Red Army was operating in that country and suffering losses'.

Back in the summer of 1941, even before Hungarian troops had joined the assault against the Soviet Union, Hungarian territory had been used as a jumping off point for Operation Barbarossa, as had Romania and German-occupied Poland. Stalin would not forget this – so far as he was concerned, the USSR's neighbours to the west were a potential threat and would need to be neutralized as part of a Soviet sphere of influence to prevent them posing a threat again. In a meeting with Anthony Eden in October 1944, Molotov told him, 'Hungary had been and always would be a bordering country. Russia's interest was therefore comprehensible. Russia did not want Hungary to be on the side of the aggressor in the future.'

Despite his agreement with Churchill, Stalin had never intended to allow the Western Allies any meaningful role in the post-war occupation and administration of Eastern Europe. Churchill and President Roosevelt would later be accused of selling out Eastern Europe to the Soviets, but in reality there was very little that could be done short of a war for which there was no appetite: by the time of the Yalta Conference, at which the future of post-war Europe was to be decided, Eastern Europe was occupied by millions of Soviet soldiers. As early as 1942, Stalin had told Molotov, 'The question of borders will be decided by force.' So far as the Soviet leader was concerned, Churchill's percentages deal was nothing more than an attempt to haggle over something which had already happened. Churchill himself entertained no illusions about Britain's ability to force the Red Army out of the territory it had occupied. Instead, he had hoped that through acceptance of the situation in Eastern Europe, he might be able to save Greece, which had been Britain's ally earlier in the war, and also preserve British influence in the Mediterranean and protect the route to Britain's empire in the Far East via the Suez Canal. Roosevelt, meanwhile, was keen to ensure Soviet cooperation in the formation of the United Nations and the new post-war settlement that he hoped would prevent another world war; he also wanted Soviet help in dealing with the Japanese forces in Manchuria and the use of bases in the Soviet Far East to support a possible amphibious invasion of the Japanese Home Islands.

Stalin's goal was to end the war having regained control of Soviet territory that had been conquered by the Germans. In addition, he wanted the territories ceded to the Soviet Union in the Molotov-Ribbentrop Pact that had been signed with Nazi Germany in 1939 (the Baltic States of Latvia, Lithuania and Estonia and parts of Finland, Poland and Romania) and a sphere of influence that covered the countries that immediately bordered the Soviet Union to the west. This, he thought, would appropriately reflect the scale of destruction and loss of life inflicted on the Soviet Union during the war. It would also help to insure the future security of his rule by preventing enemy forces from gathering on the borders of the USSR itself, as they had done in the summer of 1941. Although the Soviet excuse for denying the Western Allies any influence in the occupation of those countries in Eastern Europe that had been allied to Nazi Germany (Hungary, Romania, Bulgaria) was that the USSR had been excluded from the negotiations over the surrender of Italy, it seems unlikely that Stalin ever intended to allow anything other than Soviet domination of the region.

The German invasion had been the greatest crisis of Stalin's life. When the first news of the invasion arrived at the Kremlin, Stalin at first refused to believe that Hitler had ordered it. He suggested that it might have been a provocation by German officers and that Hitler might not be aware of it, although the formal declaration of war by the Germans later that morning soon persuaded Stalin otherwise. Although there would be a great deal of bad news over the following days, the full effects of the disaster that was befalling the Soviet Union seem to have really hit Stalin on 28 June when news arrived that the Germans had captured Minsk, 300 miles into Soviet territory. On his way out to his dacha at Kuntsevo after meeting with the military commanders, Stalin is said to have told his companions, 'Everything's lost. I give up.' The next day, Stalin did not turn up for work but stayed out at Kuntsevo and nobody could get in touch with him. Stalin did not appear the day after that either and eventually that evening a delegation led by Molotov, the secret police chief Beria and Mikoyan, responsible for trade and supply, went out to the dacha. When they arrived, according to one account, Stalin looked at them and asked, 'Why have you come?' Mikoyan believed that Stalin had thought they had come to arrest him. Instead, Beria suggested forming a State Defence Committee headed by Stalin, and Stalin agreed.

Simon Sebag-Montefiore, in his account of Stalin and his court, has interpreted this as a combination of a genuine nervous breakdown on Stalin's part and a performance, intended to test the loyalty of his followers and allow the Politburo to re-elect him to his position. Stalin seems to have been unsure of how events would unfold when his colleagues arrived and although a line was drawn under the disastrous conduct of the war until that point, the Soviet dictator would not forget what had happened or those who witnessed it. 'We were witnesses to

Stalin's moments of weakness,' observed Beria. 'Joseph Vissarionovich will never forgive that move of ours.'

Although the arrival of the Red Army in Hungary was presented as liberation by Soviet propaganda, those who witnessed it for themselves often felt it was a mixed blessing. There were immediate outbreaks of rape and violence committed against civilians by Soviet soldiers. This caused despair even among the local communists, who understood all too well how effective it would be at turning people against the Soviet system. There was also looting, both on an individual scale by Soviet soldiers and on a larger scale as official and unofficial reparations for the damage caused by the war in the Soviet Union. This was despite the destruction that had been inflicted in Budapest especially by the fighting.

Three-quarters of the buildings in Budapest had been destroyed – 4 per cent had been totally destroyed, while only 22 per cent had been left habitable. The city's population, meanwhile, had been reduced by a third. In 1945/46, Hungary's Gross National Product was half that of 1939 and 40 per cent of the country's economic infrastructure had been destroyed. When the Germans retreated, they took a large proportion of Hungary's railway rolling stock with them, and a lot of what remained would be taken by the Soviets as war reparations, or what Hungarians termed 'official looting'. According to the peace treaties that officially ended the Second World War, the Soviet Union was entitled to all the German-owned property in Hungary as compensation for the destruction that had been inflicted by the Germans. About one-third of Hungarian industry could be described in this way, with the result that 200 complete factories, together with the machinery from 300 more, were dismantled and shipped back to the USSR. Entire sectors of the Hungarian economy were taken over wholesale by the Soviets: transport, electricity, steel production, coal mining, the oil industry.

As well as reparations in kind, there were also cash payments to be made. Hungary was obliged to pay $200 million in official war reparations to the USSR, along with $50 million each to the governments of Czechoslovakia and Yugoslavia, at pre-war 1938 prices. In addition to this, the Soviets had taken one-third of Hungary's reserves of gold and silver bullion back to the USSR. A United Nations estimate suggested that 40 per cent of Hungary's national income was swallowed up by looting, reparations and other costs imposed by the Soviet occupation. Partly due to this burden, and partly to the latest in a succession of bad harvests in the countryside, the Hungarian currency collapsed in August 1945 and Hungary suffered some of the worst hyperinflation ever recorded. The crisis

The view west from Buda Castle (then known as the Royal Palace) towards Krisztina Boulevard in 1945, showing the damage that had been sustained during the fighting for Budapest at the end of 1944. (Fortepan: Glázer Attila)

A view along the eastern embankment of the Danube, showing the remains of the Margit Bridge and a number of steamers that had been sunk at their moorings. (Fortepan: Fortepan)

A man walks past one of the piers of the Lánchíd or Chain Bridge, the first permanent bridge across the Danube in Hungary. All of the bridges across the Danube in Budapest were blown up by German military engineers in the hope of slowing the Soviet advance. Note the ice on the river, which indicates that this is early 1945. (Fortepan: Glázer Attila)

Another view of the Lánchíd, looking from the eastern Pest side of the river across to Buda. This shows more clearly the thoroughness with which the German engineers had done their job in 1944. (Fortepan: Fortepan)

was only resolved when the pengő was replaced in August 1946 by a new currency, the forint, backed by $40 million in gold reserves that had been taken to Germany late in 1944 and then recovered and returned by the United States.

On 4 November 1945, Hungarians went to the polls to choose their new government. Six parties fielded candidates in the election, and of these five won seats in Parliament: the Independent Smallholders, Social Democrats, Communists, National Peasants and the Democratic Party. By far the biggest share of the vote went to the Independent Smallholders, traditional representatives of landholders and the bourgeoisie, who won 57 per cent of the vote and 245 seats. The Social Democrats won 17.4 per cent and sixty-nine seats, the Communists 17 per cent and seventy seats. This came as an unpleasant surprise to both the communists and their Soviet backers; the communist leader, Mátyás Rákosi, had predicted a triumph for his party and with a surprising degree of courage blamed the defeat on the public connecting the communists with the raping and looting of Soviet troops.

In a shattered Eastern Europe looking to rebuild itself after the destruction of the war years, communism was not unpopular with ordinary people – it was utopian and it offered an alternative to the pre-war governments that people blamed for involving them in the war. However, Hungary was not fertile ground for the communists despite the right-wing Horthy regime and the German occupation that had followed it. There were no inducements from Moscow that the party could offer the electorate to make up for the negative things with which communism and the USSR were associated. In Poland and Romania, for instance, the communists could point to favourable border changes but Moscow was unwilling to discuss a similar arrangement for Hungary. In addition to this, the communist presence in Hungary before the war had been small.

The Hungarian Communist Party had been banned by Admiral Horthy following the chaos that had resulted from Béla Kun's short-lived Hungarian Soviet Republic. However, it remained in existence unofficially and underground throughout the years that followed, re-emerging into the open following the arrival of Soviet troops and moving into new offices in central Budapest, in the building that had formerly been the Gestapo's headquarters in the city. The Kremlin also sent some 300 Hungarian communists to accompany the Red Army into the country; these so-called 'Moscow communists' (as opposed to those who had been in Western Europe or North America) were for the most part Soviet citizens, some of whom had lived in the USSR for as long as twenty years and

A worker in an apron carries a banner showing a large portrait of communist leader Mátyás Rákosi as part of a march on 1 May 1946 at Oktogon in Budapest. (Fortepan: Berkó Pál)

Rákosi campaigning during the 1945 elections in Hungary. The communists did not do as well they had led the Soviets to believe that they would. (Fortepan: Angyalföldi Helytörténeti Gyűjtemény)

lost all connection with their homeland. Their leader was Mátyás Rákosi, whose instructions from Moscow were to build a Stalinist colony of the Soviet Union in Hungary.

Rákosi, born the fourth child of twelve to a Jewish merchant in a Hungarian-speaking part of what is now Serbia, had been attracted to radical left-wing politics ever since his childhood. He had helped to found the Hungarian Communist Party in 1918 and the following year was one of the leaders of Béla Kun's Hungarian Soviet Republic. After the collapse of the Hungarian Soviet Republic, Rákosi travelled through Europe on behalf of the Comintern (the Communist International, the organization set up by the Soviet government to spread both communism and Soviet influence), but also of the Soviet secret police. In 1924, he returned to Budapest to help rebuild the Hungarian Communist Party, which had spent the past five years underground. The following year Rákosi was arrested and imprisoned, being released and allowed to travel to the Soviet Union in 1940.

While in the Soviet Union, Rákosi quickly concluded that the way to success (and indeed survival) was slavish loyalty to Stalin, a habit he would keep up – later, the Hungarian Communist Party would make no important decisions without first getting the approval of the Soviets. Rákosi would become known as one of the 'little Stalins', because of his imitation of the Soviet leader's policies, along with two others: Ulbricht, the party leader in East Germany, and Bierut, leader of the Polish Communist Party, both of whom were also Moscow communists who had survived to eventually take power thanks to Soviet help or protection.

Prior to the election Stalin's old crony Marshal Voroshilov, the chairman of the Allied Control Commission that represented the three victorious powers in the country, had already announced that whatever the results of the voting, the coalition government that been in office since the end of the war would remain in place. Negotiations between the political parties eventually produced a government approved by the Soviets in which the communists held three ministries and Rákosi took the office of Deputy Premier.

To start with, the communists were good democrats and helpful coalition partners. They helped to repair churches that had been damaged during the fighting and Ernő Gerő, who would later rise to become Rákosi's deputy and replacement, took proud responsibility for rebuilding the bridges across the Danube in Budapest, which had been dynamited by the retreating Germans as Soviet troops advanced through the city. The communists were also responsible for the land reform programme that distributed some two million hectares of agricultural land which had previously been part of the vast aristocratic landed estates that had dominated the countryside of pre-war Hungary among about 600,000 peasants. This policy had been implemented by the communist minister for agriculture, Imre Nagy, and gave him a popularity among ordinary Hungarians that he would never lose.

In a reckoning with the Second World War years, 279 people were hanged as war criminals; these had been leaders of the Arrow Cross movement and other prominent local fascists as well as men who had volunteered to join the SS. However, others had also been swept up in the net. Istvan Bethlen, for example, had been a member of Horthy's cabinet and had been an advocate of a separate peace with the USSR, while before the war Ivan Lajos had published the so-called 'Grey Book' in which he denounced the Nazi preparations for war; both men were deported to the Soviet Union and there disappeared.

In the summer of 1947, there were again elections in Eastern and Central Europe. In Hungary the issue hanging over the vote was the Paris Peace Treaty that had recently been signed and which allowed the Red Army to remain in the country in order to maintain lines of communication with the troops in the

Imre Nagy from his identity card in 1945, when he served as agriculture minister. (Fortepan: Jánosi Katalin)

Soviet zone of occupation in Austria. Unlike the elections of 1945, those of 1947 bore evidence of tampering. Despite this, the communists won less than a quarter of the vote in Hungary; the German and Austrian Communist parties also lost by large margins in the elections in those countries. This was despite the influence that communists wielded throughout Eastern and Central Europe by virtue of being backed by the Soviet Union and its resources, especially the Red Army.

In May 1946, Rákosi addressed the Central Committee of the Hungarian Communist Party. 'Now that communist parties have everywhere become stronger and come to the fore,' he announced, 'there should be pressure for the institution of the Communist International or some other international communist body ... whenever a country achieves the conditions for the liberation of the proletariat or for socialism, this will be carried out, with no regard for whether the respective country is in a capitalist environment or not. This is also a new perspective, which simply means that in a country where as a result of the work of the communist party these conditions are present, it has to be realized.' Marxism had always argued that there were scientific rules to history and the development of societies that made it inevitable that eventually communism would come to power; now, Rákosi was arguing, the process could be speeded up in countries such as Hungary where the communists had influence through the Russians.

What the Hungarian communists and their Soviet backers were looking to establish was a totalitarian state, in the model of Stalin's USSR. The object of a totalitarian state is to ensure that the state controls every aspect of day-to-day life, public or private. The first step in the process was to break up and remove political opposition. These were the original 'salami tactics', so-called because communist demands would at first be modest and would increase only gradually, taking over slice by slice – Rákosi himself coined the phrase in a speech in 1952. The centre-right Smallholders were the first target; twenty-four of their MPs were implicated in a fictitious plot to restore the pre-war Horthy regime, including the most formidable of the Smallholder leaders, Bela Kovacs, who was arrested in the Parliament building itself by Soviet troops and deported to the Soviet Union. In spring 1947, the Smallholder prime minister, Ferenc Nagy, left the country for a holiday. While in Switzerland he was telephoned by Rákosi, who made some dark suggestions about what would happen if he came back to Hungary and suggested he stay abroad. Nagy did not go back to Hungary.

The Social Democrats were dealt with after the 1947 elections. During the years when the Communist Party had been banned in Hungary many communists and communist fellow-travellers had joined the Social Democrats, so it wasn't too difficult to call an internal referendum on merging the party with the communists. Anyone who opposed holding the referendum was barred from voting and then expelled from the party; the merger was approved and carried out in June 1948.

1948 was the key year in the communist takeover of Hungary. In the autumn of that year, Hungary's banks were nationalized. On 28 December, all private enterprises in the country that had more than ten employees were also nationalized. Collective farms were introduced in the countryside. In 1949, Hungary was officially declared a People's Democracy. Posters and placards in the streets declared that Rákosi was 'Stalin's best pupil' and Soviet advisors were brought in to bring Hungary into line with Soviet practice in every way possible. Hungary's national flag was altered to incorporate the hammer and sickle. The education system was changed to follow the Soviet model and the only foreign language taught was Russian. The public holidays were the same as those in the Soviet Union: 25 December became Pine Needles Day. Hungary's army was issued with

1 May 1947. Rákosi is seen here at Budapest's Heroes' Square in the foreground to the left. Behind him, second from the right, is László Rajk. (Fortepan: Berkó Pál)

Soviet-made weapons and Soviet-style uniforms; even the time of the main meal in the mess was changed to follow the Soviet pattern.

Surveying the scene in Hungary before the uprising, the UN was unequivocal: 'Real power was in the hands of Mátyás Rákosi, a communist trained in Moscow. Under his regime, Hungary was modelled more and more closely on the Soviet pattern. Free speech and individual liberty ceased to exist. Arbitrary imprisonment became common and purges were undertaken, both within and outside the ranks of the Party.'

These harsher, more clearly pro-Soviet policies were being implemented across Eastern Europe in 1947 and 1948. It's normally argued that this was in response to the more determined stand that the United States was taking against the expansion of communism and Soviet influence: on 12 March 1947, President Truman had announced a programme of American economic and military assistance for Greece and Turkey, which was followed in June 1947 by the European Recovery Program, best known as the Marshall Plan after Secretary of State George Marshall, committing the US to rebuilding Europe. Although the Eastern bloc countries were eligible for Marshall aid, the presumption in Washington was that

Rákosi speaking on 11 June 1948. By this point the communists' political rivals had been elimi-
nated and they would soon begin to introduce a Soviet-style system in Hungary. (Fortepan: Rádió
és Televízió Újság)

they would be forbidden from accepting it, and that it would therefore be Stalin rather than Truman who would draw the dividing line between the Eastern bloc and the rest of Europe – an important propaganda victory. Stalin did indeed forbid the participation of first the Soviet Union and then the satellite states.

But it was not simply the Americans driving events. The elections in Hungary in November 1945 had been permitted by Stalin partly because he was confident that time was on his side and support for the Communist Party would grow, and partly in order to halt Western criticism of what the Soviets were doing elsewhere, especially Poland. However, despite all the advantages of their Soviet backing and training, the communists, as the 1947 election showed, were not popular – the 1945 result had not been what the Soviets had been led to expect, and that in 1947 was even worse. The clamp-down on Eastern Europe was a reaction to the failure of the communist parties there as much as anything else.

In following the Soviet system so closely, the Rákosi regime was creating one of the main grievances that would later be held against it. The UN would later note that 'In any study of the causes of the uprising, attention is necessarily focused on the penetration of Hungary by strong Soviet influence over a period of years. This influence was felt in the life of every Hungarian citizen.' It added, 'Resentment at alien influences was present in criticisms of the regime voiced before October 1956.'

In a largely Catholic country, it was important for the communists to remove the influence of the Church as a rival centre of authority. Cardinal József Mindszenty, Archbishop of Esztergom, had been installed as Prince Primate of Hungary, the country's senior Catholic cleric, in October 1945. A man of firm principles and indifferent to his physical safety, Mindszenty had opposed the communists and called on his fellow Hungarian Catholics to do likewise. On 26 December 1948, he was arrested. The authorities intended to make an example and a warning of him: Mindszenty was tried and sentenced to life imprisonment in January 1949. In the Vatican, Pope Pius XII excommunicated everybody who had been involved in the Cardinal's trial and conviction. Lutheran Bishop Lajos Ordass and the Greek Orthodox Bishop Janos Odon Peterfalvy were also arrested and imprisoned. From 1949 all priests in Hungary were obliged to swear an oath to the constitution and any who refused would also be imprisoned. To ram home the point, the Regnum Marianum church on Heroes Square in the centre of Budapest was torn down and replaced by a statue of Stalin, four metres high, on a limestone plinth.

Above: Cardinal Mindszenty, Archbishop of Esztergom and senior Catholic clergyman in Hungary, speaks at a Catholic school on 17 May 1947. A fervent opponent of communism, he would be arrested, tried and imprisoned by the beginning of 1949. (Fortepan: Erky-Nagy Tibor)

Right: To make their point, the communists put up a large statue of Stalin in Heroes' Square, seen here in 1951. (Fortepan: Magyar Rendőr)

Criticism of the regime became increasingly dangerous. The Hungarian secret police, the Államvédelmi Hatóság, or AVH (State Protection Authority), was notoriously effective, relying on a network of informers that may have made up nearly one in ten of the Hungarian population. The AVH had made its headquarters at 60 Stalin Avenue (now 60 Andrassy Avenue), which had once been the base of the fascist Arrow Cross movement and for eighteen months after the end of the war, the AVH had steadily recruited former members of the Arrow Cross into its ranks. Rákosi argued that these working-class fascists would be loyal to the new regime because they could be blackmailed about their past and because they could easily be gotten rid of if they were no longer required. The AVH's chief torturer, Lieutenant-Colonel Gyula Prinz, for example, had done much the same job at No. 60 Stalin Avenue when it had been the Arrow Cross headquarters. The head of the AVH, Gábor Péter, by contrast had worked for the NKVD, the feared Soviet secret police, helping to keep the European communist parties loyal to Moscow. Despite being widely loathed in Hungary, Péter's connections in the KGB's Moscow headquarters, the Lubyanka, ensured that he prospered. The AVH was key to the security of the Rákosi regime and recognized as such, so its members were among the elite of communist Hungary.

Rákosi's regime was particularly viewed as a police state from the summer of 1949. In June of that year, Foreign Minister László Rajk was arrested. Charged with attempting to overthrow the government, he was tried, found guilty and hanged on 15 October. His wife Júlia had also been implicated in the plot and was sentenced to six years in prison while their infant son was placed in an orphanage under a different name. The reality of the so-called Rajk plot was rather different. In 1948, Marshal Tito (the communist partisan leader who had taken power in Yugoslavia at the end of the Second World War) had dared to take a different line to that approved by Stalin while developing Yugoslavia's economic policy. Stalin took the resulting split between Yugoslavia and the Soviet Union personally and ordered the satellite states in Eastern Europe to conduct a purge to remove anyone who might be inclined to agree with Tito. In Hungary Rákosi took the opportunity to rid himself of Rajk, who he saw as a potential rival for the leadership and whom he deeply distrusted. Despite the fact that Rajk was as much a hardline Stalinist as Rákosi himself and, while interior minister, had been responsible for the attacks on the Churches and their leaders, he was not a 'Moscow communist' like Rákosi and had been part of the Hungarian Communist Party in its underground years.

Interior Minister László Rajk, speaking on 15 March 1947, with the Parliament building in the background. In 1949, Rajk, seen by the jealous Rákosi as a leadership rival, would fall from grace. (Fortepan: Berkó Pál)

The great purge that followed Rajk's trial and execution lasted almost three years. In that time, some 1.3 million people were prosecuted, of whom about half were jailed. A further 50,000 people were arrested but never tried. There were more than 2,000 summary executions but many more died from mistreatment while in police custody. In the towns and cities 13,000 people were classified as 'class enemies' and forced to leave their homes for the countryside, where they worked on the collective farms under close supervision. The newly empty flats and houses went to satisfy the demand for suitable homes for the new communist bureaucrats. The Hungarian Communist Party was gripped by paranoia and, just like in the Soviet Union in the 1930s, any potential foreign influence was cause for suspicion. Those who had left Hungary during the Horthy years were in danger of accusations of being Western spies, while those who were veterans of the International Brigades in the Spanish Civil War were suspected of being followers of Trotsky, that eternal Stalinist bogeyman. However, those who had stayed in Hungary and gone underground were also suspect, of being informers for the Horthy government. There didn't even have to be a reason – arrests were often made on the basis of assumptions rather than evidence and some of those picked up were simply unlucky.

Those who had not come to the attention of the secret police had other problems to cope with as well. Although living conditions in some of the Soviet bloc countries had generally begun to improve by the 1950s, those in Hungary were getting worse. In the first four years of communist rule living standards had fallen by 20 per cent at the same time as the working week had got longer. On 31 December 1951, for example, the Rákosi government had introduced new price and wage reforms that saw prices go up by as much as 20 per cent and wages fall by about the same. In addition 'peace loans' of up to 12 per cent would be taken from workers' pay packets. Although these were theoretically voluntary payments, workers who did not volunteer could be named and shamed. On the average worker's salary, it would take eighteen months to earn enough to buy a new suit or a new dress; luxuries were strictly reserved for the Hungarian elite and especially for the Soviet advisors.

Rákosi and Ernő Gerő, who was responsible for the Hungarian economy, had overseen rapid reconstruction to repair damage caused by the fighting, followed by rapid industrialization of what had previously been a largely agricultural economy, because that was what Stalin had done in the Soviet Union. Other aspects of the Soviet system were also introduced, such as Five Year Plans for economic development. Workers were paid using a piece rate system, i.e. they were effectively paid per item produced. As in the Soviet Union, a system of production norms was brought in. This meant that each worker had a personal schedule that he or she had to meet. If a worker failed to meet the norm, their wages were docked; if they exceeded their norm, workers found that targets went up, which effectively meant a pay cut. The result of this was a rapid increase in production quantities, but at the expense of quality, which quickly declined. Contracts between the Soviets and Hungarian firms were cancelled because the Hungarians were providing goods that were shoddy.

The speed of industrialization in the urban areas also worsened the situation in the countryside as many thousands of peasants left the countryside for jobs in the new factories and industrial plants that were springing up in the cities. The collective farm system that had been set up in 1948 was deeply unpopular. Peasants were forced to join the collectives and to sell their produce to the state at prices set in the Five Year Plan. Any peasants who refused to cooperate could find themselves labelled 'kulaks', another term imported from the USSR (where it referred to better-off peasants frequently accused of causing food shortages by hoarding grain, an accusation that could lead to a death sentence), and subject to the attentions of the AVH. The agricultural system began to fail and there was heavy food rationing in early 1950s Hungary.

Speaking in the months following the end of the uprising, senior figures in the Hungarian Party acknowledged that the policies followed by Rákosi and Gerő had failed. At the start of December 1956, István Dobi, chairman of the Praesidium, said: 'If in this country people have reason to complain against the inhuman character of the regime which was swept away on 23 October – and everyone knows that there was cause enough for bitterness – then the villages had many times more reason to complain than the towns. It would be difficult to say which was bigger – the stupidity or the wickedness of the Rákosi régime's rural policy.'

János Kádár, who would take charge of the Hungarian government following the end of the uprising, was also willing to criticize Rákosi. 'I can affirm, speaking from personal experience,' he said on 11 November 1956, 'there is not a single man or leader in Hungary today holding State or Party office, who would wish to restore the old mistaken policy or methods of leadership. But, even if anyone should still wish to restore the old methods, it is certain that there is no one capable of doing this; for the masses do not want the return of the old mistakes, and would relentlessly sweep from power any leader who might undertake such a task.'

In seeking to build a Stalinist state in Hungary, Rákosi took no important decisions without first consulting the Kremlin. It's difficult to know how many times Rákosi and Stalin may have met after the communist takeover of Hungary; Victor Sebestyen notes that Rákosi would holiday regularly in Crimea but that there are no records of whether he ever met Stalin, who was himself partial to holidays on the Black Sea coast, there. The Hungarian leader certainly seems to have bombarded his mentor with letters asking for advice, which were almost never answered, Rákosi taking silence to mean assent. Although many in the leadership in Budapest were jealous of Rákosi's closely guarded relationship with Stalin, it does not seem to have been particularly friendly but instead a mixture of fear and sycophancy on one side, and deep dislike on the other. Stalin appears to have had an ambivalent attitude to the fawning to which he was generally subjected by those around him, seeking adulation but holding in contempt those who obliged too eagerly. It is not difficult to imagine his reaction to Rákosi's sycophancy and to the personality cult of his own that the Hungarian leader was building up.

Having tried obsequiously to construct a model Stalinist state in Hungary, Rákosi and his colleagues had succeeded in creating what was perhaps the most oppressive state in the Soviet bloc. But on 5 March 1953 everything changed: Stalin died.

2. LIBERALIZATION AND BUILDING TENSION, 1953–OCTOBER 1956

On 13 June 1953, six weeks after Stalin's death, a delegation of some of the top members of the Hungarian government arrived at the Kremlin for a meeting. None of the Hungarians knew what they would be discussing.

A triumvirate of the secret police chief Lavrenti Beria, Foreign Minister Vyacheslav Molotov and Georgi Malenkov had officially taken power following Stalin's death but the rivalries that had seethed among the Politburo members while the old dictator was alive had broken out into the open and factions formed and dissolved as the magnates jostled for power. One thing on which they all agreed, however, was that it was vital to keep the Eastern bloc together, for ideological reasons and for the sake of Soviet prestige. At the same time, it was obvious that the bloc was fragile and that unless Moscow took steps to shore it up, it could collapse completely. Ulbricht in East Germany, for instance, had been rapidly industrializing his previously largely agricultural country; this, he was told, had to slow down. The industrialization programme was exacerbating the economic crisis that gripped East Germany, leading to large numbers of East Germans fleeing to the West and to unrest among those who remained. The Politburo was now planning to move to forestall the crisis they saw brewing in Hungary.

Rákosi had led the delegation to Moscow, along with Gerő and other ministers; the Soviets had insisted that Imre Nagy also be present but had not said why. When the meeting began, the Hungarians were faced by a Soviet delegation that included some of the major figures in the leadership at that time: Khrushchev, Malenkov, Molotov, Mikoyan and Beria. Doubtless to Rákosi's great surprise, it quickly became clear that he was the reason they were there. Beria began proceedings. 'We know that Hungary has had Habsburg emperors, Tartar khans, Polish princes, Turkish sultans and Austrian emperors,' he told Rákosi. 'But as far as we know she has never yet had a Jewish king, and that is what you are trying to become. You can be sure we will never allow it.'

Rákosi tried to defend himself but the Kremlin magnates were not interested. Briefed on the facts and figures by the Soviet ambassador in Hungary, Yevgeny Kisilev, the Politburo tore into the Hungarian leader. They insisted that things had to change, Khrushchev observing that unless the Hungarians were careful, their people would 'chase you away with pitchforks'. Molotov said: 'You have finally to understand that you cannot eternally govern with the support of Soviet bayonets.' So far as the Soviet leadership was concerned, the answer was clear: Rákosi had enjoyed absolute power in Budapest for too long and if collective leadership was good enough for the Soviet Union, it was good enough for Hungary. Rákosi could no longer be both leader of the Communist Party and prime minister, the head of government – he would have to share power and the Soviets wanted Imre Nagy as prime minister.

On 4 July 1953, Prime Minister Imre Nagy made a speech in Parliament in which he set out his policies, what he called the 'New Course'. The speech was broadcast

Imre Nagy, seen on his way back to Budapest from Moscow in June 1953, following the meeting at which Rákosi had been told by the Soviets that he would have to share power with Nagy. (Fortepan: Jánosi Katalin)

live on radio, and in it Nagy promised change: there had been mistakes, he said. Internment camps would be closed and minor political prisoners released; 'class enemies' deported from the cities would be allowed to return home; there would be no more discrimination against so-called kulaks in the countryside and farmers would be able to leave the collective farms; the system of norms in the factories would change and private enterprise would be allowed. For many of the people listening this was heady stuff and to hear it in the voice of Imre Nagy, the agriculture minister who had carried through land reform back in 1945, meant people believed it. Expectations were therefore high.

Nagy's term as prime minister lasted until January 1955. On 7 January, Nagy and Rákosi were again summoned to the Kremlin, only this time it was Nagy on the agenda. Met by Malenkov, Nagy was accused of incompetence in running the Hungarian economy and other errors. Nagy had perhaps suffered from expectations that were too high, although Rákosi had not helped, undermining the prime minister whenever possible. Although the Soviets did not fire Nagy, it was clear that he no longer enjoyed Moscow's support. This left Rákosi in a position to be able to remove his hated rival, a process he began while Nagy was confined to his home by his doctor as he recuperated following a heart attack. On 18 April, it was announced that the new prime minister was András Hegedüs, a protégé of Rákosi, now clearly back in control. There were, however, limits to his authority: Moscow had banned the personality cult that Rákosi had set up in imitation of Stalin; there were also to be no more purges or attacks on prominent Hungarians. What Rákosi could still do, and which he set about with enthusiasm, was persecute Imre Nagy. Nagy was expelled from the Communist Party and prevented from taking any paid work. He had been ordered to carry out the communist equivalent of penance – self-criticism – but refused on the grounds that he had not done anything wrong.

Imre Nagy had been a member of the Communist Party since the First World War. Taken prisoner while fighting in the Habsburg infantry on the Eastern Front, Nagy had discovered communism in a Siberian prisoner of war camp. He went on to fight for the Red Army in the Russian Civil War before returning to Hungary to work underground for the Communist Party. Arrested and imprisoned (he took the opportunity to study agriculture in his prison cell), Nagy was expelled from Hungary and from 1930 to 1945 lived in the Soviet Union. Unlike the other émigrés in Moscow, who lived and plotted together in the Hotel Lux, Nagy took a flat in the city and worked for the Moscow Statistical Office while continuing his studies in agriculture at the Agrarian Institute. During the Second World War, Nagy had tried to volunteer for a guerrilla unit that was to be dropped by parachute behind German lines but was instead assigned to work broadcasting propaganda to Hungary on the Soviet-controlled Radio Kossuth.

Following the war Nagy was appointed agriculture minister and oversaw the land redistribution that won him his initial popularity but was only in post for a year. He also served as interior minister, this time lasting less than a year. After his dismissal as prime minister, and unable to find any other work, Nagy lived quietly in Budapest. With each new punishment meted out by Rákosi, Nagy's reputation among the ordinary people of Budapest grew. He was described as being a 'good Hungarian' despite his loyalty to the Communist Party and despite his lack of skill as a politician. He apparently possessed, noted the UN, 'certain warm human qualities which appealed to the masses'. A group began to develop around Nagy: communists who favoured reform and were worried about the possibility of Hungary returning to Stalinism. A semi-official opposition to the communist government was evolving. Although Nagy remained a loyal communist despite his expulsion from the party and insisted that there should be no political activity in Hungary outside the party, he was nevertheless convinced that he would be called back to power to prove that it was possible for communism to have a human face.

In the Soviet Union, meanwhile, Nikita Khrushchev was manoeuvring his way to power. He had been promoted to the Soviet Politburo in 1935, when he became the Moscow First Secretary. He began a huge programme of rebuilding that changed the face of Moscow enormously, destroying many of the capital's old churches and helping to create the Moscow Metro. Khrushchev would also fully play his part in some of the darker aspects of Stalin's regime, ordering the arrests and executions of thousands of Party officials in the purges. During the Second World War, Khrushchev would serve as a political commissar attached to the Red Army, being present for Soviet disasters at Kiev and Kharkov, but also for the defence of Stalingrad and the defeat of the German offensive at Kursk. As the Germans were pushed back, Khrushchev took responsibility for running his native Ukraine, working with the secret police chief Beria to defeat three Ukrainian nationalist armies that were fighting Soviet troops. After this, he was recalled to Moscow to serve as one of Stalin's close advisors.

Khrushchev had orchestrated the removal of seemingly the most formidable of his rivals, Beria, in the summer of 1953. Very shortly after the meeting in the

Kremlin at which Rákosi had been told he would have to share power with Nagy, riots had broken out in East Berlin and other parts of East Germany because of the difference in living standards between East and West Germany. Soviet troops had easily suppressed the riots and Khrushchev used the opportunity to rid himself of Beria, who had suggested that the Soviet Union could tolerate a reunified, capitalist Germany if it was neutral. Over the next few years, Khrushchev continued to manoeuvre until, by the middle of 1955, he was the dominant leader in the USSR. Once he had achieved dominance, he could start to implement his ideas. Among other things, Khrushchev believed that the only way to save communism and thus to permit it to meet its goal of providing a better life for working people than capitalism was to reform the system and acknowledge the errors that it had made. This was the reasoning behind what has become known as the 'Secret Speech', delivered by Khrushchev to the Twentieth Congress of the Communist

Nikita Khrushchev, in an argument with US Vice-President Richard Nixon over the benefits of capitalism at the American National Exhibition in Sokolniki Park, Moscow, in July 1959. Khrushchev had become leader of the Soviet Union by mid-1955. (US National Archives)

Party of the Soviet Union on 25 February 1956. Officially titled 'On the Cult of Personality and its Consequences', the speech pulled no punches about Stalin.

'The negative characteristics of Stalin, which, in Lenin's time, were only incipient, transformed themselves during the last years into a grave abuse of power by Stalin, which caused untold harm to our party,' Khrushchev told his audience.

'As facts prove, Stalin, using his unlimited power, allowed himself many abuses, acting in the name of the central committee, not asking for the opinion of the committee members nor even of the members of the central committee's politburo; often he did not inform them about his personal decisions concerning very important party and government matters.'

Khrushchev would go on to expand on some of his ideas in a speech at a dinner given for him in Varna, on the Black Sea coast of Bulgaria, much later, in May 1962. 'Stalin wrote his own biography,' he announced. 'We take this biography and we see how this biography was corrected in Stalin's hand. It is shameful to correct this way. "So say the people," wrote Stalin. He wrote this about himself. This is a confusion of the great with the infamous. This is Stalin. All this was. He is a Marxist, he is a Leninist, and he was a murderer, he was capable of the greatest infamy, and he committed this infamy.'

Khrushchev's criticism of Stalin proved too much for some of his audience to cope with: Bierut, the Polish leader, died of a heart attack while reading a copy of the Secret Speech. The Secret Speech was so called because it had been delivered at a closed session of the Party Congress, with only Communist Party delegates present: the press and any other guests had specifically been excluded. Despite this, however, its text spread remarkably quickly, especially in the satellite states of Eastern Europe, where the effects were explosive. The most effective way in which news of the speech spread was Radio Free Europe (RFE), which broadcast propaganda and jazz (which had been dismissed as decadent by the communists) into the Soviet bloc twenty hours a day. Although in theory RFE was funded by a private organization called Crusade for Freedom, which held fund-raising drives up and down the United States, any donations that might be received were topped up secretly with US government funds.

Dwight D. Eisenhower was elected president in November 1952, and again in 1956, on a platform of a more aggressive policy towards the Soviet Union and the satellite states, with the ultimate aim of 'rolling back' communism. Previously, US government policy had been to try and 'contain' communism. This was advocated by George Kennan, a diplomat at the US embassy in

Moscow, first in the so-called Long Telegram (sent to the State Department from the Moscow embassy in February 1946) and later in a published journal article. Kennan argued that the Soviet government behaved as it did because it suffered from a sense of insecurity rooted in Russian history that feared foreign influence. Therefore, in order to preserve the fragile Soviet system, the Soviet Union had to be isolated from the outside world, and in order to justify this isolation, the outside world had to be depicted as hostile. Possible hostile outside influence could also be used to justify a crackdown on the Soviet population, which might also be a threat to the regime. The solution was to contain the spread of Soviet influence and therefore show the Soviet government that its strategy would not work. However, not everyone agreed with this assessment. In 1949, John Foster Dulles advocated the 'liberation' of the 'subject people'

President Eisenhower addressing the nation in 1957. Former Supreme Allied Commander Europe during the Second World War, Eisenhower won the presidency for the Republicans in the 1952 election and again in 1956. (US National Archives)

living under communist regimes, and this more aggressive strategy became known as 'rollback'. When he was elected in 1952, Eisenhower appointed Dulles as his secretary of state.

A great believer in psychological warfare, Eisenhower approved a large increase in the budget for propaganda operations against the Soviet Union, one beneficiary of which was RFE, which had the advantage of being able to deny that it was funded by the US government, thanks to the Crusade for Freedom. Despite the rhetoric, though, the old general was in fact a lot more cautious than he had appeared on the campaign trail. This caution was amplified when, in August 1953, Eisenhower was informed that the Soviets had probably developed a hydrogen bomb. Eisenhower knew from the results of tests of American hydrogen bombs what destruction could be caused by their use and quietly determined to avoid situations that could escalate into nuclear war.

RFE, meanwhile, was wildly popular in Hungary and developed a reputation for being first to broadcast news that would otherwise be censored by the authorities. One Hungarian student said of the station: 'I felt that its most positive contribution was its attempt to give a general picture of the situation in the West and the help it gave to Hungarian youth through its youth programmes, together with detailed information about the political situation, which unfortunately we could not get from our own newspapers.'

Within weeks of Khrushchev addressing the Party Congress, RFE was reporting in detail on the Secret Speech to its audience behind the Iron Curtain. In Hungary, people who had heard about Khrushchev's denunciation of Stalin began to wonder: if Stalin had been a criminal and a murderer, then what did that make Rákosi, 'Stalin's best pupil'? They did not have to wait too long to find out the answer. In accordance with the new policy from the Kremlin, the Hungarian government had tentatively begun the process of reform, albeit held back by Rákosi: the Central Committee of the Party dutifully denounced Stalin and hailed the reform movement but at the same time emphasized the need for collectivization of agriculture and the priority of heavy industry over consumer goods, both policies associated with the old Stalinist regime and both wildly unpopular. On 27 March 1956, however, the government addressed the Rajk case.

Rákosi announced that the Supreme Court had investigated the arrest, trial and subsequent execution of former foreign minister László Rajk and had concluded that the entire affair had been based on false charges concocted by Gábor Péter and his cronies in the AVH. The same conclusion applied to other cases connected with that of Rajk. Some 300 people, many of them former members of the Party and some of them former senior members, were released from prison as their convictions were deemed to have been baseless. The admission that the Rajk case, which had rocked Hungary, had been based on false charges and had led to the loss of innocent lives was a major blow to the image of the government. If this had been done to Rajk, how many of the others who had been arrested were also innocent?

Although the official line was that Péter and the AVH had been the driving force behind it, nobody believed this: Péter had himself been arrested and imprisoned in January 1953 and was clearly being used as a scapegoat. People began to criticize Rákosi openly and in public, something that previously would have been unheard of, and to call him a murderer. Pressure began to grow on Rákosi.

In March 1956, the communist youth organization DISZ (Dolgozó Ifjúsági Szövetség – the League of Working Youth) established a debating group which was to be called the Petőfi Circle. Sándor Petőfi is Hungary's unofficial national poet, a liberal revolutionary and key figure of the 1848 revolution against the Austrians who is believed to have been killed in battle against the Russian troops brought in by Emperor Franz Joseph to suppress the revolution. Organized by enthusiastic members of the Communist Party, the Petőfi Circle undermined the authority of the Party by holding debates that became huge public meetings where politics could openly be discussed for the first time since 1948. A debate on socialist science, for example, revealed the exploitation by the Soviets of Hungary's uranium deposits, much to the outrage of the audience. On 27 June 1956, the Circle nevertheless held a debate on socialist legality, i.e. the police state. One of the speakers was Júlia Rajk, László Rajk's widow, who made a blistering denunciation of Rákosi and the regime. Equally effective was a debate on 7 July on the subject of press freedom, in which Nagy's friend Géza Losonczy described to the crowd how the former prime minister had been treated by the leadership. It was estimated that between 5,000 and 6,000 people heard this debate, listening through the night to loudspeakers that had been set up in the streets. This was the first time that Nagy had been discussed in public since he had been ousted the previous year and led to what the UN described as 'an almost riotous demonstration against Rákosi and his regime, criticism being endorsed even by men hitherto regarded as reliable Party members'.

That summer the Soviets, who had been monitoring events in Hungary with increasing concern, intervened again. On 13 July, Anastas Mikoyan arrived in Budapest as the Kremlin's representative. Rákosi and Hegedüs went out to the airport to meet him. In the car on the way back to the city centre, Mikoyan informed Rákosi that it had been agreed that he was ill and that the condition was sufficiently serious that he would require treatment in Moscow. It had been decided that Rákosi had to go, and this time the Soviets intended to make sure that he could not find a way back to power. Rákosi telephoned Khrushchev in Moscow and tried to appeal against the decision, but Khrushchev confirmed that he would indeed require medical treatment in the Soviet Union. Rákosi even found himself undermined by his deputy Ernő Gerő, who had realized that this was his best opportunity to be appointed Rákosi's successor. Mikoyan reported back to Moscow that 'One can see how, day after day, the comrades are further losing their grip on power. Nothing is being done.' He also observed that 'A parallel centre is forming from enemy elements operating actively, decisively and self-confidently.'

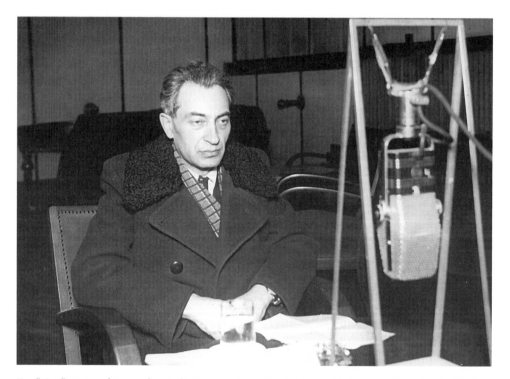

Ernő Gerő, pictured in a radio studio in 1955. In 1956, with Rákosi being forced out by the Soviets, the ambitious Gerő seized his chance to take over the leadership in Hungary. (Fortepan: Rádió és Televízió Újság)

Gerő was indeed appointed to replace Rákosi. When this was publically announced in Hungary, it came as a surprise to many as Gerő was a hardline and inflexible Stalinist in much the same mould as his predecessor. After Rákosi's fall from power, ordinary Hungarians had been hoping for a liberalization of the regime and it was hoped that Nagy, who symbolized a more liberal outlook for so many people, might return to public life. There was optimism when it was announced that General Mihály Farkas, the extremely unpopular former minister of defence under Rákosi, had been expelled from the Party. However, although Gerő brought János Kádár, an opponent of Rákosi's, into the Politburo, he also brought back József Révai, who had been Rákosi's ideological chief, and Imre Hòrváth, another friend of Rákosi's.

The Russians were not simply relying on Mikoyan's replacement of Rákosi with Gerő to keep the trouble in Hungary in check. Mikoyan had been accompanied on his trip to Budapest by a delegation from the Soviet army led by General Malinin. Part of the reason why Malinin and his men had come to Budapest was to assess the plan that had been developed by the Soviet forces in Hungary in case of large-scale rioting. Moscow was anticipating that a more forceful remedy might be required if the political solution did not solve the problem.

On 6 October 1956, László Rajk was reburied in a public ceremony that was watched by 100,000 people lining the streets of Budapest. The date was symbolic – the anniversary of the execution of thirteen Hungarian generals by the Austrians after the revolution of 1848. After the ceremony, a group of about 500 students marched to the monument to Count Batthyány, the first prime minister of Hungary, who had also been executed by the Austrians on 6 October 1849, the same day as the thirteen generals. There, they shouted slogans against the communists until the demonstration was broken up by the police.

Gerő had at first been against the idea of a reburial for Rajk but he had changed his mind after being persuaded that it would be a good opportunity to show how the government was changing. He had not attended the ceremony himself as he was out of the country for much of September and the first week of October – like Rákosi, Gerő had a taste for arranging meetings with the Soviet leadership in Crimea, where he could enjoy a holiday afterwards on the sunny Black Sea coast. Gerő would later tell the new Soviet ambassador, Yuri Andropov, that it had been a mistake to be away when Rajk was reburied, but he then left again to spend a week in Yugoslavia, meeting with Tito and enjoying another holiday on the Dalmatian coast, away from autumnal Budapest. Andropov wrote despatches

The reburial of László Rajk on 6 October 1956. A huge crowd gathered at Kerepesi Cemetery to witness the ceremony. (Fortepan: Berkó Pál)

Another view of the crowd gathered at Kerepesi Cemetery for the reburial of László Rajk, this time from behind a group of men in uniform (presumably members of the AVH or police) watching the crowd. (Fortepan: Berkó Pál)

back to Moscow in which he despaired of how complacent Gerő seemed to be in the face of the mounting tension in Hungary.

By the time of the Rajk reburial, there was a general feeling among Hungarians of disillusionment about the Gerő regime. The UN noted that 'A glance backward over the year 1956 in Hungary leaves the impression of an element of hopefulness, tending to disappointment as the rehabilitation of Rajk and the dismissal of Rákosi both failed to bring about far-reaching changes.' It is often said that the most dangerous moments for dictatorships and other repressive governments come when they become more liberal and less repressive. Hungary was not so relaxed that it could satisfy the demands for change and reform that were now becoming increasingly popular and thus relieve the pressure that was building up but it had relaxed enough that people were no longer afraid, as they had been previously.

When, less than a week after the reburial of László Rajk, the news broke that General Farkas and his son Vladimir, an AVH officer, had been arrested, there were calls for them to receive public trials – a sign both of the lack of faith that those making this demand had that the government would take action which indicated a real break with the past and of their confidence that they could safely make such a demand without fear of retribution. Suspicions were not allayed by the announcements that Imre Nagy had been reinstated in the Party and that he would also be reinstated to his University Chair – Nagy had not, people noted, been invited to join the government.

Even opponents of the uprising, the UN would observe, agreed later that the situation in Budapest in the days leading up to 23 October was tense, with the potential to become very dangerous.

3. UPRISING PART ONE, 23–29 OCTOBER

On 23 October 1956, the Chinese Foreign Ministry in Beijing received a telegram from its embassy in Budapest. The Chinese diplomats reported that 'This afternoon, Budapest university students organized a demonstration attended by tens of thousands in support of the Polish events; their slogans were "independence, freedom, democracy".'

The 'Polish events' that the Chinese diplomats referred to had begun earlier that year. In late June 1956, there had been rioting in the city of Poznań, in the west of Poland. Although this had been easily dealt with by Soviet troops, it worried elements within the Polish Communist Party. The reform faction within the Party wanted Władysław Gomułka as leader and on 19 October 1956, Gomułka was indeed elected. This was a problem for the Soviet leadership in Moscow as under Bierut, Gomułka had been expelled from the Party for what was described as right-wing deviation and had spent time in prison; in addition to this, Gomułka's reform programme included the removal of Politburo members such as the pro-Soviet minister of defence, Marshal Rokossovsky, who had been a senior Soviet military officer during the Second World War. After Gomułka had been elected, Khrushchev ordered Soviet troops to encircle Warsaw and then flew into the Polish capital at the head of a delegation to confront the Poles. Over two days of tense talks, the Soviets and the Poles eventually reached a compromise. In exchange for guarantees by the Polish leadership that their reforms would not pose a threat to communist rule in the country or to the unity of the Soviet bloc as a whole, the Soviets pulled their troops back and accepted Gomułka's role as leader and the implementation of his policies.

The news of what had happened in Poland had something of a catalytic effect in Hungary; the two countries had felt closely linked for a long time and what seemed to be the success of the Poles in confronting Moscow raised hopes in Hungary that something similar would be possible there too.

On 22 October, a mass meeting of somewhere between 4,000 and 5,000 students and members of the faculty and staff convened at the Technological University in Budapest and would go on for some eleven hours. It was the start of the new academic year and the first order of business at the meeting was to decide whether the university should leave DISZ, the official communist youth organization, and form its own group, something that was overwhelmingly approved by those present. Although by 1956 an eighteen-year-old in Hungary would have been almost entirely educated under the communist system and although students were considered to be an elite under that system, the Hungarian students shared the grievances of the wider population as well as others specific to themselves. The meeting went on to debate some of these grievances, such as the cost of textbooks and the quality of food and housing. After this they began to discuss broader problems.

Someone in the hall brought up Gomułka and what had happened in Poland which led to demands for democracy in Hungary. Another speaker whose name is unrecorded suggested that they put together a programme for establishing democracy in Hungary and present it to the government. This programme included the withdrawal of Soviet troops from the country as their presence was felt to make a democracy impossible. The initial document put together by the students, on a sheet of paper that had been torn out of somebody's notebook, consisted of ten points but as the evening went on it eventually grew to sixteen.

Wanting to broadcast their manifesto, a delegation of students took their demands to the radio station in Budapest hoping that they would be read out on that evening's 9 o'clock news but the censor objected to some of the points on the list and, wanting to have the manifesto read out in its entirety, the students left. The editors of the DISZ newspaper, *Szabad Ifjúság* ('Free Youth'), had been at the meeting and although they offered their support to the manifesto, they also declined to publish it, fearing for their safety if they called for the Soviet troops to leave. Eventually the students decided to publish themselves, in *Jövő Mérnöke* ('The Engineer of the Future'), which was produced by students at the university. Some 2,000 copies were printed, along with many more copies of the manifesto typed out on typewriters or copied using duplicators by students and sympathetic academics and secretaries over the course of that night.

During that long meeting, it was announced that the Hungarian Writers' Union was planning to show its support for the events in Poland by laying a wreath at the memorial to József Bem, a hero of the 1848 revolution against the Austrians who had been born in Poland. The students agreed that they would mount a demonstration in sympathy. The students of Budapest University had also been holding a mass meeting that evening and it was agreed that the students of the two universities should demonstrate simultaneously, joining together to make their way to the Bem memorial. The time set for the demonstration was 3 p.m. on 23 October.

On the morning of 23 October, Gerő arrived back in Budapest from his meetings with Tito in Yugoslavia. He decided to deal with the planned student demonstrations by simply banning all public gatherings in Budapest. However, at the last minute Gerő then changed his mind and decided to allow the demonstrations to go ahead after all, influenced perhaps by concerns that the police might not be willing to use force to suppress any trouble. At 3 p.m., as scheduled, the demonstrators began to move off. In the Pest district, the Budapest University students set off from the Petőfi statue; the crowd, estimated to have been about 12,000 strong, began with moderate chants and banners, but as more people joined the demonstration and as the demonstrators grew in confidence, it became increasingly radical. In Buda, where the Technological University was based, about 8,000 people set off. It was here that one of the most famous symbols of the 1956 uprising first appeared: a green, white and red Hungarian tricolour flag with a hole in

Demonstrators on the streets of Budapest, seen here at the corner of Király Street and Erszébet Boulevard, part of the Grand Boulevard, one of central Budapest's busiest streets. (Fortepan: Pesti Srác)

The Hungarian tricolour flag with a hole in the middle where the Communist hammer and sickle symbol had been cut out became one of the symbols of the Uprising, seen on what is now János Pál Pápa Square (named after Pope John Paul II). (Fortepan: Pesti Srác 2)

the middle where the hammer and sickle emblem had been cut out, handed to the students by someone from the window of one of the flats they were passing by.

By 4.30 that afternoon, some 25,000 people had arrived at Bem Square but nobody had suggested what to do after the march and nobody wanted to leave yet so people were simply milling around. Somebody suggested that they should march to the Parliament building and the idea was enthusiastically taken up. The way to Parliament took the demonstrators through some of Budapest's major residential and commercial districts and increasing numbers of people joined them, the mood growing darker and uglier. The call from the crowds now was '*Russkik haza!*' – 'Russians go home!'

At about 5 p.m. Gerő made a phone call to Andropov, the Soviet ambassador. Andropov had seen something of the mood of the protestors and he was worried, as was the Hungarian leader, who asked the ambassador to request the use of Soviet troops to put down the protestors. Gerő then telephoned the Soviet military attaché and made the same request. Both Russians said they would do what they could to persuade Moscow. Only then did Gerő call Moscow and speak to

The chant of the protestors on 23 October was '*Ruszkik Haza!*' – 'Russians go home!' The demand is seen here painted on the window of a Budapest bookshop. (Fortepan: Pesti Srác)

Khrushchev, to whom he admitted that the situation was serious but didn't mention that he had requested Soviet troops. Khrushchev learned this from Andropov and from the minister of defence, Marshal Zhukov. Although Khrushchev said the question would have to be decided by the collective leadership, that evening Zhukov sent orders to the Soviet commander in Hungary to prepare for combat.

Meanwhile, in Budapest the crowds reached Parliament at dusk and began to demand that Imre Nagy come out and speak to them. Nagy had, at first, been suspicious of the demonstrations and wary of getting involved. He had been readmitted to the Communist Party earlier in October and was keen for his friends and supporters not to do anything that might put that in jeopardy. When he had first heard of the demonstrations Nagy had said that decisions should be made by the Communist Party (the only organization, he believed, that could change Hungary for the better), not by crowds in the streets; Nagy was also uncomfortable about how much further the students' demands went from his 1953 reform programme and worried that the situation might be a 'provocation' designed to give the authorities cause to arrest and imprison him if he became involved. Nagy therefore intended to stay at home, well away from any trouble. However, many of his friends and supporters did attend and then went to see Nagy to persuade him to go to the Parliament building and address the crowds. Nagy was at first reluctant to go but eventually his friends succeeded in persuading him and the writer Tamás Aczél, who had a car, drove the former prime minister into the city centre at about 7.30 p.m.

Earlier in the evening, a group of demonstrators had gone to the Budapest Radio building in the hope of getting the sixteen points broadcast along with news about the protests. When they arrived, they found that the radio station was under guard by almost 300 armed AVH policemen and soldiers, equipped with tear gas and machine guns. More demonstrators arrived and by about 6 p.m., there was a crowd of thousands outside the radio station, chanting slogans. The station's director, Valéria Benke, was ordered to negotiate with them and she allowed twenty demonstrators into her office, where they were watched by a dozen armed AVH men. At about 7 p.m., a mobile radio van arrived at the street outside the radio station, carrying technicians and an announcer. The announcer told the crowd that Benke had agreed to broadcast the sixteen points. If they were silent, the manifesto would be read live on air, immediately. But when the people in the flats around the radio station building turned on their radios and heard only music, everyone realized that this had only been a ploy by Benke. It went badly wrong when the protestors seized the radio van and started to use it as a battering ram to break down the gates of the building and force their way into the radio station. Budapest Radio was under siege.

At 8 p.m. Gerő came on the air. He had been due to give a speech that evening and it was hoped that this would take into account the demonstrations and the strength of public feeling and that there would be some concessions offered. Instead, Gerő's speech was uncompromising and he scolded the demonstrators. After this spectacularly ill-judged offering, the mood on the streets began to darken further.

Back at the Parliament building, Imre Nagy addressed the crowds at about 8.45 p.m. However, he too misjudged the mood of those on the streets and called on everybody to trust the government and the Party and to go home, a speech that was badly received. After he had finished his oratory, Nagy went to Communist Party headquarters, where nobody seemed to know what to do.

Crowds had been gathering in Budapest's Heroes' Square, where there were statues of some of the great heroes of Hungarian history, erected to mark the

When the statue of Stalin in Heroes' Square was pulled down, all that was left was a pair of boots standing on the plinth. A group of Hungarians is seen here affixing a Hungarian flag to the remains of the statue. (Fortepan: Pesti Srác)

Another view of the remains of the Stalin statue, with Hungarian flag attached. (Fortepan: Pesti Srác)

millennium of the Hungarian state in 1896. To these had been added a huge bronze statue of Stalin, twelve metres high and standing on a marble plinth. The removal of this statue was one of the students' demands in their sixteen points. The crowd tried to pull the statue down using ropes attached to a lorry but after several attempts had failed an engineer brought up metal-cutting equipment and this, aided by cranes from the city's tram system, eventually succeeded in bringing Stalin crashing down. The only bit of the statue that was left was the boots. Although a detachment of policemen had been sent to the square, they soon left after seeing that there was nothing they could do to stop what was happening.

The AVH policemen guarding the Budapest Radio building, however, were confident that they could get the crowd that still filled the street outside to disperse. At about 9 p.m. they threw tear-gas grenades out of some of the top floor windows and then began to fire into the crowd. 'In so far as any one moment can be selected as the turning point which changed a peaceable demonstration into a violent uprising,' as the UN later observed, 'it would be this moment.' Not long

A Soviet war memorial just off the Danube embankment that has been badly damaged and pointedly embellished with the date '1956'. (Fortepan: Pesti Srác)

after, AVH reinforcements arrived at the radio station in ambulances and were attacked by the crowd who took their weapons. The demonstrators were now armed. Soldiers were rushed in to reinforce the AVH but after a moment's hesitation they sided with the crowd.

Word of what was happening in the city centre had by now made its way out to the working-class districts of Budapest like Csepel and Újpest and workers began to make their way into the city centre by truck, carrying weapons that they picked up along the way from policemen or army barracks or munitions factories. By 11 p.m. there was firing on the Budapest Radio building. The midnight news reported incidents at several points in the city.

That evening, the Politburo met in Moscow to discuss the situation. Zhukov gave a synopsis, describing the demonstrations and the clashes at the radio station in Budapest, as well as the occupation of the government and Party buildings in the city of Debrecen in the east of Hungary. Khrushchev then made the argument in favour of sending in Soviet troops, which the majority of the Politburo was in favour of. Kaganovich and Zhukov both made the point that the situation in Hungary was nothing like that in Poland: 'The government is being overthrown,' said Kaganovich, a hardliner. The only one who disagreed was Mikoyan, who argued that they should try 'political measures' before sending in troops, suggesting re-appointing Imre Nagy. 'The Hungarians themselves,' Mikoyan said, 'will restore order on their own.' Although Khrushchev agreed that they should 'recruit Nagy for political action', he also thought that Soviet troops should be deployed, to make sure of regaining control over the situation. A report to the Politburo on 24 October recorded: 'In accordance with the decision of the Minister of Defence Marshal Zhukov, Soviet troops crossed the Hungarian border. In all there were 128 rifle divisions and 39 mechanized divisions, which began to enter Hungary at 2.15 at the points Csop, Beregovo, and Vylok.'

The intervention of Soviet forces had two major consequences for the uprising. Firstly, it prolonged the fighting. Before the intervention of the Soviet army, only the AVH had been willing to use force against the demonstrators and freedom fighters; neither the regular police nor the Hungarian army was willing to do so. Without the arrival of Soviet troops, it was felt, the situation in Budapest would have returned more or less to normality within a few days. Secondly, it changed what was happening from an attempt by Hungarians to force their government to change to a fight against an oppressive occupying foreign power.

Tanks and trucks outside the AVH building on Jászai Mari Square. (Fortepan: Pesti Srác)

By the early hours of 24 October, the demonstrators outside the radio station had successfully forced their way into the building and occupied it, only to be driven out again. A crowd of demonstrators had also been fired on by AVH guards outside the offices of the Party newspaper *Szabad Nép* but once armed demonstrators arrived at the newspaper, they overwhelmed the AVH and took control of the building.

Soviet troops were first seen in Budapest at about 2 a.m. on 24 October, heading through the suburbs in the direction of the city centre. Once there, they occupied the bridges across the Danube, the embankment and major buildings in the Pest district of the city on the east bank of the river, where the Parliament and other government buildings were located. The UN reported several incidents of Soviet troops opening fire without warning that morning, two of which were reported by a former Smallholder MP who claimed to have been an eyewitness: at 9 a.m. two Soviet tanks driving toward Marx Square opened fire at people passing on the street, killing two; at 11 a.m. a Soviet tank outside the Western Railway Station shot a soldier who was talking to a civilian. The UN also reported that

that morning had seen the first recorded incidents of Hungarian civilians using Molotov cocktails (glass bottles filled with petrol or another flammable liquid that once alight will seep through gaps in the armour of vehicles such as tanks; the name comes from the war between Finland and the Soviet Union in the winter of 1939/40) to attack armoured vehicles on the streets of Budapest. 'The Soviet forces had been given to understand that their task would be the liquidation of counter revolutionary gangs,' the UN observed. 'The situation in which they found themselves was that they were confronted by the unanimous opposition of an outraged people.'

Despite reporting on various disturbances in the city during the night of 23 October, the radio made no mention of actual fighting until early the following morning. An announcement broadcast at 4.30 a.m. said: 'Fascist, reactionary elements have launched an armed attack on our public buildings and on our armed security formations ... Until further measures are taken, all meetings, gatherings and marches are banned ...' Later broadcasts of this announcement replaced 'Fascist' with 'Counter-revolutionary'. At 8.13 a.m. it was announced that Imre

T-34 tanks guarding the Margit Bridge. (Fortepan: Házy Zsolt)

Tanks parked on Honvéd Street, just off Szent István Boulevard, near the Margit Bridge. (Fortepan: Pesti Srác)

Nagy had been brought back into the government as chairman of the Council of Ministers, although it wasn't made clear whether he had been made prime minister. Half an hour later a statement purporting to be signed by Nagy was read out. This announced: 'The Council of Ministers ... has ordered that summary jurisdiction shall be applied throughout the country to acts calculated to overthrow the People's Republic ... Crimes in the categories coming under summary jurisdiction are punishable by death. This order comes into force immediately.' It was only at 9 a.m. that it was announced that Soviet forces had become involved. The government, this broadcast said, had been caught unawares by 'the dastardly armed attack of counter-revolutionary gangs' and 'have therefore applied for help to the Soviet formations stationed in Hungary under the terms of the Warsaw Treaty'.

As Imre Nagy had not been a member of the government on 23 October, many people realized that despite the implication of these broadcasts, he could not have been responsible for inviting the Soviet troops as there simply would not have been enough time for them to have arrived by the time that people were waking up on the morning of 24 October. Nagy had in fact been told at midnight that he had been appointed prime minister; he immediately accepted the role. He was then told to sign the written invitation for Soviet troops to restore order, which Moscow had insisted the Hungarian government provide, but refused. The invitation was political cover for an intervention the Soviet government had already agreed to make. He did, however, sign the declaration of martial law that was then announced on the radio at 8.45 that morning.

At the meeting on 23 October, the Politburo had not only decided to send troops to Budapest. Zhukov had suggested that a member of the Politburo should go too, to serve as the Politburo's eyes on the ground. Khrushchev agreed and decided to send two: Anastas Mikoyan and Mikhail Suslov. Mikoyan, born in Armenia, had been a Bolshevik since 1915 and developed a reputation for being very shrewd and a survivor; he operated at the highest levels of Soviet politics from Lenin's day through to the Brezhnev era in the mid-1960s. Mikoyan also had a reputation as a natty dresser, having developed a taste for business suits on a trip to the US while responsible for trade and supply during the 1930s. Suslov by contrast had achieved power after the war, becoming the Politburo's expert on ideology and international relations. Before that he had been responsible for running deportations in the Caucasus region and then dealing with anti-Soviet resistance in the Baltic States after they had been captured by the Red Army. Mikoyan and Suslov flew from Moscow to Budapest and on 24 October they sent back their first report. 'We were accompanied by tanks,' they said of their trip into the city centre, 'because there was shooting in Budapest at this time and casualties on both sides, including Soviet soldiers and officers ... On the streets together with the Soviet troops were Hungarian patrols. In contrast to Buda, where it was calm, there was continuous shooting in Pest between isolated groups of provocateurs and individuals and our machine-gunners, beginning at the bridge and extending to the Ministry of Defence building, as well as toward the Central Committee building. Our men did more of the shooting; to solitary shots we replied with salvos.'

On the morning of 24 October, the freedom fighters in Budapest were still relatively few in number although they were well armed, having acquired weapons from police stations, armaments stores and from Hungarian soldiers both on the streets and in barracks. By the end of the day, their number would have swelled to about 3,000, of whom approximately eighty had been killed and another 450 wounded. The Chinese embassy reported back home that the freedom fighters were using the offices of *Szabad Nép* as well as other facilities to publish appeals to the general population: 'We are armed! The fight must be continued in the interest of attaining our freedom and independence! The police and army are with us! We call upon every Hungarian so that we go on a general strike! Until the government caries out our demands, until the murderers take responsibility, the Hungarian people respond with an immediate general strike!'

The fighting between the freedom fighters and the Soviet troops was fluid, groups of Hungarians forming to fight isolated skirmishes and then dispersing again afterwards. However, there were four main strongpoints held by the freedom fighters in the city. These were Széna Square in Buda, Tompa Street and Báross Square in Pest and the Corvin Cinema. The freedom fighters at the Corvin Cinema were among those who were able to hold out for the longest as it was almost a perfect stronghold for them. A strongly built circular building in the Pest area of the city, it stands where three roads meet, including Üllői Avenue, along which Soviet troops coming from the east needed to travel in order to reach central Budapest and objectives such as the Parliament building, the Soviet embassy, Communist Party headquarters and the Danube bridges. With four-storey buildings on all sides, the cinema was difficult for Soviet tanks to get close to; as soon as Soviet armoured vehicles turned out of the side streets surrounding the cinema and onto the main road, they were within range of a heavy gun that had been taken from a disabled Soviet tank and mounted in the cinema doorway. And as if all this was not enough, behind the cinema was a fuel pump with which glass bottles could be filled to make Molotov cocktails.

Near the Corvin Cinema on Üllői Avenue could be found the Kilián Barracks, formerly known as the Mária Terézia barracks. Hoping to deny the building to the freedom fighters, senior army officers ordered Colonel Pál Maléter to hold it. Arriving with five tanks commandeered from an armoured regiment, Maléter took one look at the situation and decided that he would go over to the rebels. The fighting that developed between the Soviet soldiers and the Hungarian freedom fighters on 24 October was particularly intense around the Corvin Cinema and the Kilián Barracks.

Despite their overwhelming superiority in firepower, the Soviet troops in Budapest soon found themselves in trouble. Soviet tanks found it difficult to manoeuvre in the narrow streets and could easily be outflanked and ambushed by the highly mobile freedom fighters, while the Soviet commanders were unwilling to face the heavy casualties that would result from using their infantry

One of the main roads in the vicinity of the Corvin Cinema. To the right, on the corner of Üllői Avenue, can be seen the Kilián Barracks. An insurgent with a rifle slung over his shoulder can be seen at bottom right. (Fortepan: Pesti Srác)

A T-34 tank of the Hungarian Army. Although the majority of the rank and file were in favour of the uprising, its senior officers were pro-Soviet. (Fortepan: Pesti Srác 2)

to clear the streets or from using their superiority in artillery and other heavy weapons. The UN also reported that some of the Soviet soldiers were less than enthusiastic about the task that they had been assigned, as those Soviet troops who had been stationed in Hungary for some time prior to the uprising had built up friendly relations with locals. Russian had, since the communists took power in 1948, been the second language taught in Hungary so it was not difficult for Hungarians and Soviets to communicate; there must have been some embarrassment when it became clear to the Soviet troops that they were regarded as oppressors rather than liberators and that the people they were fighting against were ordinary workers and students, not fascists.

At midday Imre Nagy addressed the nation live on radio but again failed to correctly judge the mood of his audience. Appealing for calm, he offered an amnesty to all those who would stop fighting and return home. Nagy, despite his good intentions, was still looking to resolve the problems that he had identified back in 1953 when he had first been appointed prime minister and had not yet realized

A notice in Russian headed: 'Soviet Soldiers!' It goes on to appeal to the Soviet troops not to shoot. (Fortepan: Fortepan)

Right: A history of resistance: Countess Ilona Zrínyi (1643–1703), Hungarian noblewoman and heroine of the anti-Habsburg uprising of 1683–88, by Károly Jakobey (1826–91).

Below: Artist August von Pettenhofen's interpretation of the opening session of the Hungarian parliament in 1848, the year of revolutions across Europe. Hungary was at the forefront.

Army officers of the Hapsburg Austro-Hungarian empire, 1848.

Mihály Munkácsy's striking artwork: Seated in an inn, a pale young man wearing remnants of a military uniform describes to his companions a battle, which occurred in 1848 during the Hungarian uprising against Austrian-Hapsburg domination. An international figure, Munkácsy trained in Budapest, Vienna, Munich and Paris. While attending the 1867 Exposition Universelle, he met the French realist Gustave Courbet and several members of the Barbizon school. Many of his later years were spent in the village of Barbizon, where he produced scenes of contemporary life set in his native Hungary or in France. Striving for realism, he frequently used photographs in composing his scenes.

Budapest in the nineteenth century, when the Hapsburg empire was still one of the great powers of Europe. This Photochrom image shows what is now Blaha Lujza Square, not far from the east bank of the Danube. (Library of Congress)

Another Photochrom image of nineteenth-century Budapest, this time looking towards what was then the Franz Joseph Bridge from Buda on the west bank of the Danube. The Franz Joseph Bridge is today known as Szabadság (Freedom) Bridge. (Library of Congress)

Appointed by Rákosi to succeed Imre Nagy in early 1955, András Hegedüs (right) would serve both Rákosi and Gerő as prime minister, lasting in office until Imre Nagy was re-appointed at the start of the uprising. He is seen here at a ceremony on 1 May 1955. (Fortepan: Fortepan)

The former Yugoslav embassy where Imre Nagy sought asylum in 1956. He was executed two years later. (Photo Aled Betts)

An American propaganda poster used in Italy, highlighting the contrast between Khrushchev's criticism of Stalin in the Secret Speech and his suppression of Hungary. 'We are all Stalinists,' the poster has the Soviet leader declare. (US National Archives)

A flag from the 1956 Hungarian Uprising on the memorial to the victims located outside the Hungarian Parliament. (Photo Ian Pitchford)

The 1956 Uprising Memorial in Budapest. (Photo alex.ch)

Above and below left: A ceremony of remembrance at Plot 301 in Budapest's New Public Cemetery, where Imre Nagy and other figures executed after the uprising were buried. This took place in 1988, a year before the reburial of Nagy and the others. (Fortepan: Hodosán Róza)

The 1956 Hungarian monument in Budapest Park, Toronto. (Photo GDT Aquitaine)

AZ 1956. OKTÓBER 25 -I
VÉRES CSÜTÖRTÖK
ÁLDOZATAIRA EMLÉKEZVE
A TÚLÉLŐK

Bullet holes as a memorial to the 1956 Uprising by sculptor József Kampfl, Kossuth Square, Budapest. (Photo Yamen)

that the situation he was facing in October 1956 was dramatically different. As Victor Sebestyen points out, although it was often claimed that Nagy was being held prisoner by Gerő and the AVH, he was rather 'a prisoner of his own mind'. Needless to say, the armed freedom fighters ignored his offered amnesty.

By the morning of 25 October, there was a feeling of exhilaration among the insurgents that they had managed to survive against the strength of the Soviet army. The only thing that united the disparate bands fighting the Russians was a desire to force the Soviet army out of Hungary. The mood was very different on the other side. At about 9 o'clock that morning, Mikoyan and Suslov arrived at Communist Party headquarters on Akadémia Street. So far as they could see, the Soviet Union had become involved in what might soon become a war to prop up the collapsing communist regime in Hungary and they were determined to exercise some control over the situation before things deteriorated too far and show the hapless Hungarian party leaders who was in charge. Ernő Gerő bore the brunt of their bad mood. Mikoyan bluntly told Gerő that so far as he was concerned, all the problems they were facing in Hungary were down to Gerő; Suslov wondered aloud whether Gerő should simply resign. Gerő tried to defend himself by telling the Kremlin's emissaries that Khrushchev had told him that he was needed to hold the Hungarian party together but the exasperated Mikoyan snapped back at him that thanks to his efforts, the Hungarian party had fallen apart already. Mikoyan and Suslov got what they wanted: Gerő was replaced as leader of the Hungarian communist party by János Kádár. One of the demands that had been voiced immediately before the start of the uprising had been that Kádár should have more influence in the government – he had expressed support for changes in the government and had condemned the AVH for its brutal behaviour. That having been said, like Nagy he was a loyal, long-time member of the Party despite having been imprisoned and tortured by the AVH in the purge that had followed the Rajk trial.

Meanwhile, a group of about 800 people had assembled outside the Hotel Astoria and set off for the Parliament building. On the way, they were fired on by Soviet tanks outside the Western Railway Station (the Nyugati) and retreated. Back at the Astoria, the demonstrators began to ask Soviet troops stationed there (there were half a dozen Soviet tanks and other armoured vehicles outside the hotel) why they were firing on unarmed people. Eventually one of the Soviet tank crews said they agreed with the crowd's demands and that they should all go to the Parliament together. When this group arrived back at Parliament, a crowd

János Kádár, seen in 1950 at the event where the communist youth group DISZ was formed. (Fortepan: Magyar Rendőr)

estimated at some 20,000 had assembled, waiting for Imre Nagy to appear. As the tanks appeared in the square, decorated with Hungarian flags, the shooting started. Some accounts suggest that the AVH men on the roof of the Agriculture Ministry fired first when they began to worry that the crowd was going to attack the building. Other accounts suggest that Soviet troops were the ones to open fire first when the tanks that had arrived with the demonstrators also exchanged fire with other Soviet tanks that came up from the surrounding streets. Some accounts specifically blame the KGB chief, General Ivan Serov, who had also come from Moscow to Budapest. In this interpretation of events, Serov was in Communist Party headquarters when the demonstration in Parliament Square was reported to him and went off to see for himself. Serov, it is said, was especially irate about reports describing fraternization between Hungarian students and Soviet soldiers and ordered the officer in charge of the Soviet troops to clear the square. Casualties, many of them women and children, were estimated at up to eight hundred.

Tanks on guard at the Astoria intersection. (Fortepan: Kurutz Márton)

A crowd protesting outside the Parliament building. (Fortepan: Nagy Gyula)

Protestors gather outside the US embassy in Budapest on 25 October after the shootings in Parliament Square that day. (Fortepan: Nagy Gyula)

Reports of the killings in Parliament Square spread through the city, along with rumours that people had deliberately been gathered together and then herded into the square to be killed in cold blood. People began to protest outside the US legation and the British embassy, asking for aid. Many others went to the nearest group of armed insurgents, got a weapon and began fighting the Soviets and the AVH. Their numbers swelled by this inflow of new recruits who were often teenagers of school age, the insurgent groups increasingly began taking the fight to the Soviet troops. Some insurgent leaders had no problem with sending teenagers out to fight, while others were appalled by the idea of children dying in battle. Still using their successful hit-and-run tactics, the insurgents mounted more attacks against the Russians and also began to capture and hold more strongpoints in the city; these were often small squares that could easily be defended or areas of narrow streets that it would be difficult for the Soviet tanks and other armoured vehicles to enter. In the hilly streets of Buda, on the west bank of the Danube, insurgents would lay fabric on the roads and soak it in soapy water so that the Soviet tanks would not be able to move properly. In the squares, bricks placed on the road and covered by wooden sheets looked like landmines, which stopped Soviet tanks and rendered them vulnerable to attack from the windows above with grenades and Molotov cocktails. The strongest of the strongpoints remained at the Corvin Cinema and the Kilián Barracks, where disagreements that had broken out between the professional soldier Pál Maléter at the barracks and the insurgents in the cinema were put aside when word arrived of the killings in Parliament Square.

Gergely Pongrácz, who would later become leader of the insurgent group based at the Corvin, said that Parliament Square had changed everything: the Soviets and AVH had shown no mercy so the insurgents would have to show that they wouldn't be intimidated. It would not be long before Maléter and the Corvin group had the chance to show that they had not been cowed as Soviet tanks moved into position to launch an attack on the barracks and the cinema. The result was the biggest battle so far in the uprising but the Soviets were pushed

A boy standing on Tompa Street with the wreckage of a police Csepel van behind him. Many of the insurgents were teenagers. (Fortepan: Fortepan)

A barricade at Móricz Zsigmond Circle made with cobblestones torn up from the street. (Fortepan: Fortepan)

Another barricade of cobblestones at Móricz Zsigmond Circle, this time with a sign in Hungarian, repeated in Russian, saying, 'Russians go home!' (Fortepan: Fortepan)

back, leaving behind Soviet equipment and even heavy armoured vehicles for the insurgents and their allies.

Back on Akadémia Street, the Communist Party old guard were still in residence in party headquarters, egging on the Russians to take a hard line and suppress the rising by force. The resentful Gerő was trying his best to undermine Nagy and although Suslov and Mikoyan were rapidly losing patience as the Hungarian party leaders bickered among themselves, they did not yet trust Nagy enough to feel they could give him a free hand. Mikoyan in particular was unhappy that Nagy had mentioned the withdrawal of Soviet troops and told the Hungarian that he should have discussed it with Moscow's representatives first. The absolute red line so far as the Soviet government was concerned was to ensure that Hungary remained within the Soviet sphere of influence. Nagy's response was to tell the two Soviets that if the government didn't take the initiative, it would be beaten. The prime minister had decided that he had to make a clean break by removing the old guard still lurking in Akadémia Street and setting up a new government of liberal communists and non-communists but he needed the approval of Mikoyan and Suslov first. The two Soviets agreed to the new government but warned Nagy not to go too far. Nagy's friends, who were more in touch with the prevailing mood in the city, warned the prime minister that what he had agreed with the Soviets would not satisfy the insurgents.

By 26 October, Mikoyan and Suslov were beginning to express doubts about Nagy in their communications with Moscow. Although, in a meeting with the prime minister, the Soviet emissaries had approved the new cabinet and several new policies such as pay rises for Hungarian workers, they nevertheless reported that they had again warned Nagy not to discuss in public the possibility of Soviet troops withdrawing completely from Hungary and warned that a withdrawal of Soviet troops would lead inevitably to American troops entering the country, something that Moscow would not tolerate.

The following morning, 27 October, there was little shooting in the city as the curfew was lifted for the first time since the uprising had started to allow people to go out and get food. As the Hungarian communist regime had collapsed in the face of the uprising, the food distribution system that the regime had set up to supply the cities collapsed too. Fortunately for the citizens of Budapest, farmers in the Hungarian countryside showed their support for the revolutionaries in the city by bringing food into the capital and giving it away for free. As well as food, there were newspapers: some were old names that had suddenly taken a very different tone since the uprising and some were new publications that had been started to take advantage of the new freedom.

Later that morning, Nagy publicly named his new government. As he had agreed with the Soviets, this new government was a mixture of communists (including several of the Stalinist wing of the party) and non-communists such as Zoltán Tildy, who had been president of Hungary between 1946 and 1948, Béla Kovács, who along with Tildy had been one of the leaders of the Independent Smallholders, and Ferenc Erdei of the National Peasants. Among the communists was Ferenc Münnich, who had become good friends with Imre Nagy when they had both been living in Moscow before the Second World War and who had been Hungary's ambassador first to Moscow and later Belgrade. Nagy had brought Münnich into the government in the hope that his friend would be able to help negotiate with the Soviets, especially Serov. Unfortunately for Nagy, the announcement of his new government did not have the effect that he had hoped it would, resulting in protests and complaints from revolutionaries both in Budapest and in the provinces. It was too little, too late, so far as the revolutionaries were concerned.

The revolutionaries in Budapest would have other things to think about that day. At midday on 27 October, Soviet tanks and artillery were again seen moving towards the Kilián Barracks and the Corvin Cinema. When Pál Maléter had arrived at the Kilián Barracks at the start of the uprising, there had been some 900 conscripts from the Hungarian military engineers in the barracks, but Maléter had ordered them to posts elsewhere in Budapest and the barracks was now occupied by 150 trained regular soldiers and some tanks. The regular soldiers were reinforced by insurgents from the Corvin, ready to fight with Molotov cocktails or as snipers. The result was one of the most intense battles yet in the uprising. Shelling of the area by the Soviet troops damaged at least six buildings nearby as well as smashing most of the windows in the barracks. Around twenty Hungarian soldiers and insurgents were killed. On the Soviet side, there were six deaths and four tanks were destroyed. The insurgents also managed to disable an armoured car and set on fire a lorry that was carrying supplies. The Soviets withdrew.

Late that evening, Nagy held a meeting in his office with his advisors and they debated what to do next. Nagy had concluded that the moderate course he had been trying to follow since he was appointed simply wasn't working. He decided that he would have to accept the insurgents' demands if he was going to lead the revolution rather than just follow along behind. At about midnight, Nagy met

Looking down Üllői Avenue with the Kilián Barracks on the left. One of Pál Maléter's T34 tanks can be seen by the barracks. (Fortepan: Nagy Gyula)

A Soviet BTR-152 armoured car on fire on the corner of Akácfa and Rákóczi streets. (Fortepan: Házy Zsolt)

with Mikoyan and Suslov. The prime minister was hoping to be able to arrange a ceasefire. Kádár, who was also at the meeting, supported this idea and argued that following a ceasefire a political deal could be struck that would involve disbanding the AVH, an amnesty for the insurgents and discussions over the long-term future of Soviet troops in the country. The Hungarians were told that a ceasefire would require Khrushchev's approval.

What Nagy and Kádár were not told was that before agreeing to a ceasefire, the Soviets had decided on one last major military attack on the rebel strongholds in Budapest. Nagy only discovered this when he was woken at 6 a.m. on 28 October and told that the Soviet troops were taking up their positions prior to the attack. More than fifty Soviet tanks were on the move that morning, along with supporting artillery. The primary targets, as so often before, were the Kilián Barracks and the Corvin Cinema but the Soviets also planned to attack insurgents in Boráros Square near the Western Railway Station and Tűzoltó Street near the National Museum. Soviet commanders believed firmly that if one or more of these strongpoints fell, the insurgents' morale would collapse and the uprising would melt away. Both the Soviet commanders and senior Hungarian officers were keen for Hungarian troops to join in the attack. However, more junior officers were worried that the attack risked heavy loss of life and in the end no Hungarian troops joined the Soviets.

After he had been woken with news of what the Soviets were planning, Nagy spoke on the telephone to Andropov at the Soviet embassy, then to Mikoyan and finally to Khrushchev in Moscow. He told each of the Soviets that if the attack went ahead as planned, he would resign as prime minister. This was a serious threat as at this point in the uprising backing Nagy still seemed like Moscow's best hope of resolving the situation peacefully. Eventually, the Soviet troops launched only a half-hearted attack and in fierce fighting with the insurgents and soldiers lost another three tanks. The highly embarrassed Soviet commanders then withdrew their troops and agreed to the ceasefire. Both the Soviet commander in Hungary, General Laschenko, and his deputy, General Malaschenko, blamed the Hungarians. They blamed the Hungarian army for its refusal to fight alongside them and they blamed the officials of the Hungarian communist party for lacking the will to stay in power. They also blamed the politicians in Moscow for imposing too many limits on them. On the ground the Soviet troops were simply relieved that the fighting was over – they were now cold, tired and hungry. Food had been a particular issue as lack of supplies meant they were forced to forage. In a city like Budapest, this meant going into shops to look for food, which left the Soviet troops vulnerable to attack by the insurgents. Radio Free Europe and other media outlets suggested that Soviet troops were deserting to join the insurgent forces although there doesn't seem to be any evidence that this was actually the case. That having been said, some Soviet officers seem to have suspected that some of their men did not have the stomach for what they were being asked to do.

In Moscow, the Politburo too agreed to the ceasefire in Budapest. There was a great deal of argument first in which the hardliners such as Voroshilov and Molotov had argued for what they called 'decisive action'. Mikoyan and Khrushchev, on the other hand, were arguing for a Poland-style solution that would keep Hungary in the Soviet bloc while allowing more independence and the possibility of Soviet troop withdrawals. Defence Minister Marshal Zhukov

A Soviet BTR-152 armoured car on Akácfa Street, covered in chalked Hungarian graffiti. (Fortepan: Fortepan)

Passers-by examine the 122mm gun from a Soviet ISZ-3 tank that has been left behind on József Boulevard. (Fortepan: Nagy József)

agreed, suggesting that the Soviets should be flexible and consider the withdrawal of troops from Hungary if necessary. Suslov, who had been summoned from Budapest, advised that Nagy be allowed time to form a stable government, so long as it remained essentially communist. 'There is no alternative to supporting Nagy,' he told his colleagues. 'We must.' The Soviets did not have a clear plan in mind for what they wanted to happen in Hungary – all in the Kremlin agreed

Two 85mm anti-tank guns left behind on Práter Street, surrounded by a crowd of curious onlookers. (Fortepan: Pesti Srác)

that it was unacceptable for Hungary to leave the Soviet bloc but they disagreed on how far they were willing to compromise with the Hungarians to reach a solution. In the end, Khrushchev said that they would go along with the ceasefire but that the Hungarians should not go too far.

Back in Budapest, the ceasefire was announced to the population on the radio that afternoon. There were celebrations, but they were muted as nobody was sure whether the ceasefire would actually hold. At about the same time, Nagy was meeting with Mikoyan again. Nagy demanded of the Soviet envoy more freedom in dealing with the Stalinists from the Hungarian communist party who were still haunting the party headquarters on Akadémia Street and Mikoyan agreed. Gerő and his allies were put on a flight to Moscow at such short notice that they barely had time to pack. Nagy and Mikoyan moved on to go over a speech that Nagy was due to give; Mikoyan seemed perfectly satisfied with the text and reassured the Hungarian that Moscow had confidence in him.

Meanwhile, the Soviet government had another problem to deal with. The UN Security Council was due to discuss the situation in Hungary and the Soviets

An odd-looking scarecrow made from various pieces of Soviet military equipment, including a helmet and several ammunition belts. (Fortepan: Fortepan)

Above and below: The population of Budapest took advantage of the ceasefire to bury their dead. These two memorials are seen in Harminckettesek Square and the Károlyi Park. (Fortepan: Pesti Srác and Pesti Srác 2)

Another memorial, this one involving the old pre-Communist Hungarian flag. (Fortepan: Pesti Srác)

needed the written invitation for their troops to restore order in Hungary, which they still did not have, in order to avoid being labelled as aggressors and accused of acting illegally. Andropov was ordered to get a signature on the backdated letter of invitation. First, the ambassador approached Nagy, who refused to sign on the grounds that he had not been prime minister at the time. Eventually, Andropov got Hegedüs to put his signature on the invitation before the former prime minister left on the same flight to Moscow as Gerő.

Early the next morning, 29 October, there were some minor skirmishes but the ceasefire held. At dawn, the Soviets announced that their troops would be withdrawing from Budapest. They had lost 500 of their number in the fighting; twice as many Hungarians had also died. The withdrawal of Soviet forces was vital if the new Hungarian government was to be able to restore order to the country as the armed insurgent groups had stated that they would not lay down their weapons until the Soviets had agreed to pull their forces out of Hungary. Nagy now moved from Communist Party headquarters to the Parliament building, walking

Men buying newspapers on Rákóczi Street. A wide range of new newspapers came into being during the two weeks of the uprising. (Fortepan: Pesti Srác 2)

A box for collecting donations from passers-by, presumably to help the insurgents or their families. The box was on Kálvin Square, outside the Hungarian Writers' Union. (Fortepan: Papp István)

casually through the city streets. It was his first time in the fresh air since he had arrived at the Akadémia Street headquarters on the night of 23 October. His priority would have to be restoring order as soon as possible. The prime minister had ringing in his ears Mikoyan's warnings that Moscow would not tolerate a resumption of fighting by either the insurgents or the Hungarian army.

Nagy's solution to the problem was to set up a National Guard, under the command of former Budapest police chief Sándor Kopácsi, that would include the army, the police and the insurgents. The commander would be Béla Király, a hero of the fighting in the Second World War. The biggest problem that faced Kopácsi and Király was of course negotiating with the insurgents. The insurgent groups did not have any sort of central command so each insurgent leader could only control the parts of the city occupied by his fighters. Insurgent groups did not trust each other and often disagreed among themselves – factionalism was a major issue. Their sense of exhilaration over what they had achieved was also an issue as it blinded them to what might be possible in the future: what could they not do now that they had forced the Soviets to withdraw? A sense of wild optimism was in the air and many of the insurgents believed that Nagy's agreement with the Soviets was a starting point for future negotiations with Moscow. Nagy, who had considerably more experience of the men in the Kremlin than the insurgents did, was convinced that they already had the best deal they were likely to get.

What doomed the idea of an agreement between the USSR and Hungary similar to that that had been reached between the Soviets and Poland was the inability of the Nagy government to rein in the insurgent groups and disarm them.

4. UPRISING PART TWO, 30 OCTOBER–4 NOVEMBER

30 October was the start of the second week of the Hungarian Uprising. At first it seemed as though the omens were good. Soviet troops were streaming along the roads away from Budapest, watched with loathing by the civilian population. Although the guns of the Soviet tanks were ready for action, the crowds generally seemed content to simply watch them go and although there were a few incidents, no bloodshed resulted. That morning in the Kremlin a declaration had been signed that seemed to guarantee everything that Nagy could have wanted from Moscow: it promised the withdrawal of Soviet troops from Budapest and negotiations over the withdrawal of Soviet forces from elsewhere in Hungary and from the other Warsaw Pact countries too. It even admitted to previous mistakes made in Moscow's relations with the satellite states and acknowledged that they had a right to national sovereignty. Despite sounding impressive, the declaration had in fact been drawn up for possible use in Poland at the time of the rioting there earlier in 1956 that had led to the establishment of the Gomułka government. Not having been needed then, it had been edited for use with the new Hungarian government.

At a Politburo meeting that morning, even the hardliners had apparently accepted that the USSR should come to an agreement with the Hungarians to avoid further embarrassment. Molotov, for instance, advocated an appeal to the Hungarians 'so that they promptly enter into negotiations about the withdrawal of troops'. They were even prepared to contemplate the complete removal of Soviet troops, so long as the government in Budapest kept Hungary in the Soviet bloc. 'We must search for other modes of relations with the countries of people's democracy,' said Yekaterina Furtseva, First Secretary of the Moscow Communist Party. 'Anti-Soviet sentiments are widespread. The underlying reasons must be revealed,' said Dmitri Shepilov, one of the Communist Party's leading ideological experts. But, he argued, 'The foundations remain unshakable.' Defence Minister Zhukov told his colleagues that Hungary was 'a lesson for us in the military-political sphere'. Khrushchev summed up by saying

The headquarters of the Budapest branch of the Communist Party, on what is now János Pál Pápa Square. (Fortepan: Nagy József)

that the USSR should choose the withdrawal of troops and negotiations over an outright military occupation.

Who knows how things might have turned out had this positive mood prevailed? However, later that day things changed yet again. The building that served as the headquarters for the Greater Budapest branch of the Communist Party had been under guard by both Hungarian and Soviet soldiers. Unfortunately, after the withdrawal of the Soviet troops under the ceasefire agreement the building had been left unguarded. There was an argument about food supplies and a group of insurgents entered the building and recognized AVH men who had taken refuge inside. An exchange of gunfire followed, and a siege that lasted several hours and ended in a fight that led to the death of a western journalist in the crossfire and the fatal wounding of Imre Mező, the leader of the Budapest party, who was a supporter of Nagy and a close friend of Kádár. Twenty-three AVH officers were killed by a crowd that had assembled outside the Party head-quarters, including a conscript who was barely twenty and was photographed hanging upside down from a tree while the crowd kicked him. This deeply unset-tling photograph would be one of the factors that convinced the Politburo to intervene again in Hungary.

Imre Nagy had declared on 28 October that the AVH would be dissolved once peace had returned. However, the secret police had made itself so unpopular that the government had to dissolve it the day after the announcement had been made. Ivan Serov, the Chairman of the KGB, who had accompanied Mikoyan and Suslov from Moscow, drily noted that 'the morale of the operative staff [of the AVH] declined'. 'The Dep. Minister of Internal Affairs Hars came to our advisor,' Serov wrote in his report to the Politburo in Moscow, 'wept, and stated that the employees of the security organs are considered traitors, and the insurgents are considered revolutionaries. He conversed with Comrade Kadar on this issue. However, he did not get a comforting answer.'

At about noon that day, Cardinal Mindszenty, who had been jailed ever since January 1949, was released from his imprisonment in a castle north of Budapest by soldiers from the Hungarian Army. The Cardinal's first impulse was a trium-phant return to Budapest but the soldiers were ordered by the government to instead escort Mindszenty into the city early the following morning. It was feared the ceremonial entry into the city that the Cardinal had wanted might lead to more violence; Nagy and those around him were also all too aware that it would be seen in Moscow as highly provocative given Mindszenty's previous opposition to communist government.

However, Nagy proved willing to run the risk of provoking Moscow in other ways: that afternoon, he announced that the one-party system had been abol-ished in Hungary. A new cabinet of six was named: three communists, two for-mer members of the Smallholders' Party and one former member of the Peasants' Party. Although Nagy knew that this would be more than Moscow was willing to stomach, he was equally convinced that he would be swept away himself unless he kept up with the revolutionaries. Within an hour of making his announce-ment, Nagy was swamped with demands that he go further, many of them utterly

impractical. A delegation from Győr arrived in the prime minister's office insist-
ing on free elections being held within three months and then demanded that
Nagy withdraw Hungary from the Warsaw Pact, a very dangerous step that he
was not yet willing to countenance.

It did seem as though Hungary was now becoming a multi-party democracy
again. It was recognized, however, that things would not be able to go back to how
they had been before Rákosi had taken power. Bela Kovacs of the Smallholders'
Party said that the old world of 'aristocrats, bankers and capitalists' had gone for
good. The newly legal political parties proved hugely popular, with long queues of
people waiting to join. Faced now with the task of reinvigorating the Communist
Party in the face of competition that it had not seen for eight years, Kádár had to
accept that the number of genuine communists in Hungary was far smaller than

A Soviet BTR-40 and T-54 tank on the streets of Budapest, 31 October 1956. (Fortepan: Pesti Srác 2)

had previously been thought as those who had joined because they had to left for parties that better suited their opinions.

In Moscow that night, Khrushchev would be awake until the early hours of the morning as he tried to decide what to do about the deepening crisis in Hungary. Mikoyan and Suslov had been appalled by the violence that had erupted at the Budapest party headquarters. 'The political situation in the country is not getting better,' they reported back to Moscow. 'It is getting worse.' They were now starting to fear the worst and reported to Moscow that the Hungarian Army might go over as a body to the insurgents. 'It could happen,' they said, 'that the Hungarian units sent against the insurgents could join these other Hungarians, and then it will be necessary for the Soviet forces to once more undertake military operations.' They also reported that 'The insurgents declare that they will not give [their weapons] up until the Soviet troops leave Hungary.' It was looking increasingly plausible, they thought, that Hungary might leave the Soviet bloc. Khrushchev knew that the Hungarian crisis had placed him in a dangerous position as his enemies among the Kremlin magnates would not hesitate to take advantage of anything they perceived as weakness or a mistake.

On the morning of 31 October, Khrushchev called the magnates into the Kremlin to make a final decision on Hungary. He told them that he had realized that the decision he had come to the previous day had been a mistake practically as soon as he had made it. Hungary raised a challenge, Khrushchev said, and the Party, the army and the security services in the USSR would not understand if it went unanswered. Demonstrations had been reported in Poland, where the Soviets had already intervened earlier that year, in Czechoslovakia and there had been protest marches in Romania. Khrushchev also expressed concern that perceived weakness in Hungary could lead to a loss of Soviet influence (influence that would be replaced by that of the West) in both the Middle East and Eastern Europe: 'We would then be exposing the weakness of our positions ... To Egypt they will then add Hungary.' (On 30 October, Britain and France had issued the ultimatum that would lead to their joint invasion of the Suez Canal Zone.) It was even feared that events in Hungary might influence dissident movements and cause trouble within the Soviet Union itself. Although maintaining both Soviet prestige and the Soviet bloc in Eastern Europe were important, internal Soviet politics was also a factor. As Khrushchev had already spoken to the most influential of the magnates beforehand and got their approval for intervention, the only question that remained to be answered was who would be put into power in Budapest as Nagy's replacement. One candidate was Nagy's friend from Moscow, Ferenc Münnich, well known from his days as Hungarian ambassador to Moscow as being pro-Soviet. Rákosi, Hegedüs and Gerő were all in favour of Münnich taking power. The alternative was János Kádár, who was starting to appear unhappy about the direction events were taking. Even at this stage, the Politburo was willing to consider a role for Nagy: 'If Nagy agrees, bring him in as dep. premier.'

Khrushchev asked Marshal Konev, Commander-in-Chief of the Armed Forces of the Warsaw Pact and, like Zhukov, a veteran commander from the Second World War, how long it would take to defeat the insurgents in Budapest with all necessary forces. Three days, Konev told him. The timing was fixed so that everything would be finished before the celebrations to mark the anniversary of the Russian Revolution on 7 November. Khrushchev then moved to ensure the support of the other communist leaders. First would be the Chinese. Liu Shao-qi had been in Moscow for talks over the past few days and he and Khrushchev had discussed Hungary during the night of 30/31 October. Vice-chairman of the Chinese Communist Party's Central Committee, Liu was second in rank only to Mao himself. Although relations between China and the Soviet Union were starting to deteriorate, Mao was still a respected figure in Moscow and his opinion was considered important. Khrushchev met Liu at Moscow airport, just before Liu returned to Beijing, in order to ensure that he got the news promptly. During the previous night's conversation, the two had agreed to wait and see but once Khrushchev had told him of the Soviet change of plan, Liu said that overnight Mao too had decided that it was necessary to use force. Having got Beijing's agreement, Khrushchev then began a tour of the Eastern European capitals, in secrecy, to ensure that the Hungarians were not tipped off as to what was about to happen.

Khrushchev's first stop was to the far west of the Soviet Union, where he met Gomułka near Brest, just across the border from Poland. Poland was still considered to be a potential source of disruption by the Soviets and Khrushchev wanted to make sure that the action he was about to take in Hungary would not cause trouble to flare up again. Gomułka did not like the Soviet plan although he had warned Nagy that he should not go too far and did not consider him to be an effective politician. Despite his objections, however, Gomułka decided that it was best not to antagonize Moscow and agreed that he would not say anything about

Hungary in public. The other Eastern European leaders that Khrushchev met, worried about the instability that events in Hungary might cause in their own countries, were considerably more supportive of the Soviet plan than the Poles had been. Khrushchev's last stop was a meeting with the leader of Yugoslavia, Marshal Tito. Khrushchev, joined by Malenkov, travelled from Sofia in Bulgaria to Tito's holiday house on the Adriatic island of Brioni on the evening of 2 November. Having recovered from the aftereffects of the bad weather that had plagued their flight and the onward journey out to the island by boat, the two Soviet magnates spent the rest of the night in discussions with Tito. The Yugoslav leader, it turned out, accepted that the use of force could not now be avoided; like Gomułka, Tito had warned Nagy that he was going too far and had been ignored by the Hungarians. They then thrashed out between them who the next leader in Budapest would be. Tito pushed Kádár's candidacy, saying that Hungarians would identify with him as he had spent time in prison. Khrushchev had been in favour of anointing Münnich, whom he knew from the 1930s, but was swayed by Tito's argument: it would be Kádár.

Meanwhile, in Budapest the cabinet had met on the morning of 31 October. Reports were starting to come in that fresh Soviet troops were entering Hungary, crossing the border from the Ukraine. Not yet certain what might be happening, the government imposed a blackout on reporting Soviet troop movements to avoid causing panic or any incidents that would definitely lead to a Soviet subjugation of Hungary. Later that morning, Nagy and his ministers went to say farewell to Mikoyan and Suslov who were heading back to Moscow. Both the Soviet representatives had already been told that the USSR was planning to crush the uprising but both acted as though nothing were amiss. Nagy asked them about the reported troop movements but was told breezily that they were routine. Mikoyan and Suslov confirmed that Moscow was willing to negotiate the terms of the Warsaw Pact and Soviet troop withdrawals and then they left.

Despite the ceasefire and withdrawal of Soviet troops from Budapest, Nagy's position was still not yet secure. The revolution in Hungary was taking an increasingly anti-communist tone and Nagy had long been a loyal member of the Party, so the insurgents distrusted him. There was also the problem that Nagy had been following the revolution rather than leading it, which made it seem as though he had little power to shape events. When some of the leaders of the armed groups

Soviet troops on the move through Nyugati Square, outside the Western Railway Station, on 31 October 1956. (Fortepan: Pesti Srác)

Rebel corpses, 30 October 1956. (Fortepan: Nagy Gyula)

A Soviet T-54 tank drives through Oktogon as Soviet troops withdraw from Budapest. (Fortepan: Pesti Srác 2)

in Budapest met with Nagy in his office, not all of them acknowledged his authority as prime minister.

That night there was dancing in the streets of Budapest as people celebrated their newfound freedom.

As 1 November dawned, more reports were coming into the prime minister's office that Soviet troops were crossing the borders from Ukraine to the east and from Czechoslovakia to the north. Furthermore, what was known of their movements suggested that they were aiming to isolate Budapest. On 30 October the Soviets had begun an airlift using various airports and military airfields in Hungary that they had occupied. Ostensibly, this was part of the withdrawal of Soviet forces from the country: the aircraft were evacuating soldiers wounded in the fighting, and the families of Soviet soldiers and civilian personnel who had been based in Hungary prior to the start of the uprising. However, it was said that they were also bringing military supplies into the country. As October turned into November, the Soviets were carrying out three kinds of troop movements in Hungary: a public withdrawal of forces, a deployment of fresh troops intended to help the withdrawal of Soviet forces and a massing of armoured forces intended to crush the uprising once and for all.

In the early morning of 1 November, the outraged Nagy called Moscow to try and get an explanation for the flood of Soviet troops into Hungary but could get no response from the Soviets (Khrushchev at this point was leaving for Poland). Nagy's next step was to call in Andropov. The prime minister told the Soviet ambassador that he had received reliable information that fresh Soviet troops had entered Hungary and stated that this was in violation of the Warsaw Pact. Andropov, who was aware of what was being planned, played for time by saying that he didn't know what was happening and would have to ask Moscow. Later that morning, Andropov told Nagy that the troops were to protect Soviet civilians in Hungary and to relieve those that had been in combat. Nagy made a formal protest and threatened that Hungary might withdraw from the Warsaw Pact and declare neutrality. The prime minister and his aides had decided earlier in the day that they would take the step of withdrawing from the Warsaw Pact if the reports of a fresh Soviet invasion were true but Nagy was hoping that things would not have to go so far. Later again on 1 November Nagy told Andropov that he had written proof that more Soviet soldiers had crossed the frontier and informed the ambassador that therefore Hungary was immediately withdrawing from the Warsaw Pact. Andropov was invited to attend a cabinet meeting where this would be confirmed. Informing Moscow of what had happened in this meeting, Andropov noted Nagy's 'rather nervous tone'. The prime minister reported to the cabinet that he had 'demanded' an explanation from the ambassador of Soviet troop movements in Hungary and Tildy (the Smallholder former president) suggested that the government wanted to avoid 'the workers' anger turning against the Soviet Union', i.e. a resumption of armed conflict in Budapest. Andropov again played for time but Nagy told him that he hadn't answered the question. Nagy then 'proposed that, since the Soviet Government had not stopped the advance of the Soviet troops, nor had it given a satisfactory explanation of its actions', the cabinet should confirm Hungary's withdrawal from the Warsaw Pact and declaration of neutrality. Other foreign embassies in Budapest were also informed of the government's declaration of neutrality. Kádár, Andropov noted, was reluctant to support Nagy.

Murder of a communist.

Despite this declaration of neutrality, the Soviets continued to build up their forces in Hungary. It's been suggested that the Hungarian declaration of neutrality helped to decide the Soviets in favour of military intervention. Although the formal declaration only came after the Soviets had made their decision, they knew that it was becoming increasingly likely as the tone of the uprising became increasingly anti-communist and Hungary leaving the Soviet bloc was a line that could not be crossed so far as Moscow was concerned. By 2 November, it was estimated, there could have been as many as 200,000 Soviet soldiers in the country, along with up to 4,000 tanks. By the evening of the next day, Budapest had effectively been sealed off from the rest of the country except by telephone: the roads and railways had all effectively been cut by the Soviet forces. Imre Nagy was continuing his negotiations with the Soviets for a complete withdrawal of their forces and hoped that the Soviet troops were only present as a show of force to help strengthen Moscow's position in the talks. The prime minister had already decided that if the Soviets did resort to force and suppress the uprising, he would not order the Hungarian army to fight: resistance would be futile and would only lead to heavy civilian casualties which Nagy wanted to avoid. There had still been nothing in the newspapers about the Soviet troops moving towards the Hungarian capital but the news spread via rumour nonetheless. Many preferred to ignore the rumours, though, and convinced themselves that the revolution had succeeded.

Damage caused by the fighting in Rákóczi Street. (Fortepan: Pesti Srác)

People walking past the bullet-holed façade of No. 11 Erzsébet Boulevard. (Fortepan: Pesti Srác)

The Hungarian government had carried out a reshuffle on 3 November, several of the communist members being dismissed. The new government included János Kádár, despite the fact that he had apparently disappeared; he had not been seen in Budapest since 1 November and not even his wife knew where he was. Authority rested with the revolutionary and workers' councils that had been formed throughout the country as the authority of the communist government had collapsed in the face of the protests of 23 October. Councils had taken over local government and had also appeared in the army, various government departments and organizations like the radio as well as factories, mines and other industrial facilities. Intended to protect workers' interests and give the workers a voice in management, the councils wielded considerable influence and had demanded elections and the withdrawal of the Soviet troops. There was a great deal of hope in Hungary that these demands would come to pass and that life would soon return to normal. After the ceasefire, the population of Budapest began to clear up the debris of the fighting and assumed that on 5 November, a Monday, everybody would go back to work as normal as the strikes came to an end and everyday life would resume. Although there had still been no official information from the government about the Soviet troop movements, almost everyone in Budapest now knew that the city had been surrounded, although there were no signs of panic. There were even some members of the government who were optimistic about where things might be headed. The Soviet grip, however, was tightening around the Hungarian capital, and now around some of the provincial towns as well.

The talks to negotiate the departure of Soviet troops began on the morning of 3 November and by that evening it appeared that the negotiations for the withdrawal of Soviet forces had very nearly been successfully completed. The Hungarian negotiators had tried to be as accommodating as possible toward the Soviets. A Hungarian delegation led by the minister of defence, Pál Maléter, promoted to general, was invited to the Soviet military command at Tököl that night to settle the final details that remained. The Soviet officers threw a banquet in honour of their Hungarian counterparts; at about midnight the festivities were interrupted by the arrival of Ivan Serov accompanied by a group of KGB officers to arrest the Hungarian delegation. The Soviet commander, General Malinin, at first looked indignant at this interruption but then Serov whispered into his ear, after which the general shrugged his shoulders and ordered the rest of the Soviet military delegation to leave the room. Serov then placed the Hungarians under arrest.

A crowd looking into a damaged shopfront on Kossuth Lajos Street. By early November, people in Budapest were hoping that things would soon return to normal. (Fortepan: Pesti Srác)

That night, reports came into the Parliament building in Budapest that the Soviet troops were now advancing on the capital. Since he had heard nothing from Maléter and the others at Tököl, Nagy assumed that the negotiations for Soviet withdrawal were continuing and ordered that the Soviet troops not be resisted to avoid any provocations. These instructions were not changed until the early hours of 4 November, after it was announced that a new Hungarian government had been formed by János Kádár.

When the Communist Party leader broadcast on the morning of 4 November he told those listening that he and three other former members of Nagy's government had left because of its inability to deal with the prospect of counter-revolution and that the new government was intended to defeat 'fascism and reaction'. Although intended to sound as though it was being broadcast live from within Hungary, Kádár's speech was in fact pre-recorded. He had not been heard from since 1 November, when he had announced that the Communist Party was to be re-formed as the Hungarian Socialist Workers' Party and that it would take a very different approach to that of its predecessor. The new party, he said, would

97

operate 'not by slavishly imitating foreign examples, but by taking a road suitable to the economic and historic characteristics of our country'. Kádár then called on the other parties to 'overcome the danger' of foreign intervention.

Kádár's announcement on the night of 1 November had, however, also been pre-recorded. Not long after the speech began, he was picked up from his home by car along with Ferenc Münnich and taken to the Soviet embassy. Münnich had concluded that the Soviets would forcibly suppress the uprising sooner or later and wanted to be on the winning side, and he set out to persuade Kádár to do like-wise. It took Münnich a day and a half to persuade Kádár to meet Andropov and even when the time came Kádár was still reluctant to go. At the Soviet embassy, Andropov set out to flatter and charm Kádár but also told him in no uncertain terms that if he did not cooperate with the Soviets, he would suffer the same fate as Imre Nagy. Eventually Kádár agreed to go to the Kremlin and meet with the Soviet leadership. He and Münnich were taken to the Soviet military airfield at Tököl, where they were joined by Serov. At dawn they were flown to Moscow. Kádár would spend the next day having meetings in the Kremlin although

With crowds gathered, Soviet tanks have just crossed one of the bridges over the Danube, 31 October 1956. The lighter-coloured vehicle on the pavement is an ambulance. (Fortepan: Nagy Gyula)

Khrushchev and Malenkov were away, still meeting with the Eastern European leadership. Once Khrushchev returned from Brioni with Tito's agreement it was confirmed that Kádár would succeed Nagy although some of the hardliners in the Kremlin tried to suggest that Rákosi be re-installed as Hungarian leader.

Kádár was informed formally on 3 November that he would taking over, with Münnich as his deputy. He was then briefed on the Soviet invasion plan. Khrushchev told Kádár, 'We welcome your choice.' The Soviet leader also declared that 'We cannot regard I. Nagy as a Communist,' and said that unless Nagy was 'forced into retirement, he'll be working for the enemy'. Interestingly, Khrushchev's speech criticized the Hungarian leadership before the uprising, describing Rákosi and Gerő as 'honourable and committed communists' but damning Rákosi as 'hardline' and the unfortunate Gerő as 'hapless'. 'Some of the rebels are not enemies,' Khrushchev noted. 'They were antagonized by the mistakes of the leadership.' And he suggested that the Soviet leadership had erred in not making sure of the effectiveness of the leadership in Budapest. Kádár too suggested, although more diplomatically, that the Soviets had erred in only dealing with a small cabal within the Hungarian Communist Party. The new Hungarian leader was keen to make sure that his friends in the Kremlin understood that things going forward could not be the same as they had been: 'This government must not be puppetlike, there must be a base for its activities and support among workers. There must be an answer to the question of what sort of relationship we must have with the USSR.' Khrushchev agreed that the new government should not appear to be a Soviet puppet but then dictated to Kádár who the members of his government would be. Various key documents for the first days of the new government were drawn up by the Soviets in Russian and translated into Hungarian later. Kádár was also told that he would not be taken to Budapest until several days after the Soviet attack on the city; for the first few days, the city would be under the control of the Soviet army. Kádár did, however, get his way when he insisted that Rákosi and Gerő be forbidden to return to Hungary.

Budapest had effectively been surrounded by Soviet forces from 9 p.m. on the evening of 3 November and the Soviets began to advance on the city, with about 150,000 troops and 2,500 modern tanks along with air support. A further 20,000 Soviet troops had been deployed along the Austrian border to prevent Western intervention. By about 3 a.m. on 4 November, the Soviet tanks were reported to be moving into the city itself, taking up positions to cut the industrial districts of Csepel and Újpest off from the city centre. At 4.25 a.m., the Soviets opened fire on the barracks at Budaőrsi Avenue, in the south of Buda. Shortly after that artillery fire was heard throughout the city and the outlying areas. At 5.20, Imre Nagy spoke on the radio: 'Today at daybreak Soviet troops attacked our capital with the obvious intention of overthrowing the legal Hungarian democratic government. Our troops are in combat. The government is at its post. I notify the people of our country and the entire world of this fact.' Not long after this broadcast, the Nagy government contacted Cardinal Mindszenty to warn him that his life was in danger. The cardinal left his palace and went to the Parliament building, and then headed from there to seek asylum at the US legation.

In some places, the advancing Soviet forces were able to capture and hold their objectives relatively easily, for example the Danube bridges or the square outside the Parliament building. Organized city-wide resistance came to a halt after the radio station fell to the Soviets at about 8 a.m. The last broadcast made was an

A Soviet T-34 tank moves along Üllrői Avenue, watched cautiously from the window by this photographer. (Fortepan: Fortepan)

Crouching behind cover, a figure watches a Soviet ISU-152 assault gun drive past. (Fortepan: Fortepan)

appeal from the Hungarian Writers' Union at 7.57, repeated in English, German and Russian: 'We appeal for help to writers, scholars, writers' associations, academies, scientific organisations and the leaders of intellectual life all over the world ... Help Hungary! Help the Hungarian people!' The broadcast ended, 'Help! Help! Help!' At 8.07, the radio went off the air. In an appreciation of the situation at noon on 4 November, Marshal Zhukov felt confident enough to declare that Soviet forces had 'broken the resistance of the insurgents'.

Although organized resistance had come to an end, fierce fighting continued through the city as the Hungarian forces occupying various strongpoints fought on until they ran out of ammunition. Almost from the start of the Soviet attack on Budapest there had been fighting at Üllői Avenue, at the Kilián Barracks and at the Corvin Cinema among other places in Pest, and on Gellért Hill, at the Citadel and at the Southern Railway Station in Buda. The cinema for example was described by Zhukov as 'large hotbed of resistance'. The marshal reported that its defenders had been given an ultimatum to surrender and when this was refused, an attack had been launched. Similarly, the Kilián Barracks was subjected to a three-hour assault and an aerial bombardment but managed to hold out for three days. At the Citadel, too, Hungarian forces held out until 7 November. Initially, Soviet troops concentrated on attacking fortified strongpoints in the hope that when these fell, order could quickly be restored in the city. However, as the strongpoints held out and the fighting continued, the Soviets dealt with the sniper fire and other harassing attacks that they were coming under by having tanks move along the main streets firing into the houses in order to subdue the civilian population. On Soroksári Avenue, which joins Csepel and the Tököl military airport to the city centre, Soviet troops were able to establish a presence relatively easily, but suffered heavily from insurgent attacks and retaliated with assaults of their own in the side streets around Soroksári Avenue. A lot of damage was caused to buildings and there were civilian casualties, especially as it was reported that Soviet troops would fire indiscriminately, hitting a queue outside a bakery on 4 November, for instance, and an ambulance on 7 November. By the evening of 7 November, the fighting in Budapest had become intermittent and largely concentrated in the industrial districts on the outskirts of the city.

In these districts, such as Csepel, Újpest and Pestszenterzsébet, resistance continued until as late as 11 November, the local factory workers holding on tenaciously in the face of Soviet attacks. Soviet armour was faced with insurgents armed with anti-tank guns and other pieces of artillery, machine guns and grenades. There was constant harassment of the Soviet troops by the insurgents, who would resist the Soviet advance for as long as they could and then withdraw, regroup and move through the streets to attack the Soviet troops at a more vulnerable point. As in the city centre, the Soviet response to the war of attrition that was being waged in the industrial districts was to open fire on the buildings from

The collapsed front wall of a building on Baross Street. (Fortepan: Pesti Srác)

which attacks were being launched and this caused very heavy damage; some tenement buildings and other blocks of flats collapsed as a result of the damage from Soviet shells, trapping residents who had been sheltering in the cellars underneath the rubble.

The Csepel district was of particular importance to the Soviets as it was on the way to Tököl airport and they had to control the area to secure their link to the airport, where their headquarters was based. It had been argued in Csepel that as the Soviet forces were so strong that they were certain to win eventually, they should not be resisted, but this was rejected. Well supplied with weaponry, the local insurgents were determined to fight. The result was that between 4 and 9 November there was near-constant fighting in Csepel between the Soviets and the insurgents. Determined to take control, the Soviets ordered an artillery barrage on Csepel on 7 November but the resistance continued. Two demands from the Soviets that the insurgents surrender also produced no result, despite the fact that the second (on 9 November) warned that unless there was a surrender, the Soviet forces would spare no one. After the rejection of the second demand for

Resistance fighters catching up on sleep, 2 November 1956. (Joop van Bilsen / Anefo)

Damage inside a flat on Üllői Avenue. (Fortepan: Fortepan)

Very heavy damage to a building following fighting on Móricz Zsigmond Circle. (Fortepan: Fortepan)

surrender, Soviet artillery fire on Csepel intensified, as the Soviets also began firing rocket artillery into the area. At 6 p.m. on 9 November, the local revolutionary council decided that it had to surrender: the insurgents were running out of ammunition and the indiscriminate Soviet artillery fire had caused huge damage.

Outside the capital, there was more of a mixed picture. In some parts of Hungary, the insurgents had been unable to obtain arms because there had

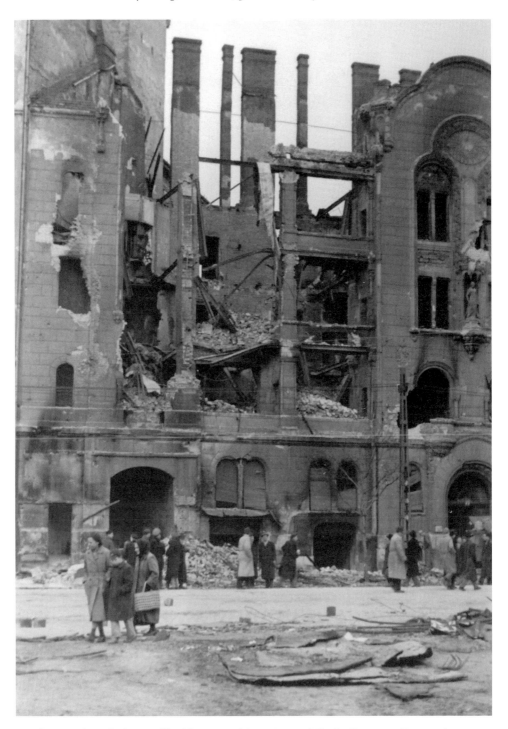

Another very heavily damaged building on Móricz Zsigmond Circle. (Fortepan: Fortepan)

A light dusting of snow on the ruins of a building on Üllői Avenue. (Fortepan: Nagy Gyula)

been no sympathetic garrisons of Hungarian soldiers, or because Soviet officers had acted to prevent them from going over to the insurgents at the beginning of the uprising. In Pécs in the south of Hungary, when it became obvious that the Soviets would move to take back control over Hungary, the local insurgents decided to abandon the city so that it would not be destroyed in fighting with the Soviets and based themselves in the surrounding hills instead. The insurgents in the hills eventually numbered in the thousands and although they suffered quite heavy casualties, it was a lack of ammunition that eventually forced the survivors to try and escape across the border into Yugoslavia. It was reported to the UN that wounded insurgents who were brought down from the mountains in Red Cross ambulances were being executed on the way to hospital, a witness reporting that two wounded fighters were executed in a town square by Soviet troops. At Székesfehérvár, Hungarian soldiers who had sided with the Nagy government broke through a Soviet encirclement and also made for the mountains, setting up bases there and carrying out a guerrilla campaign against Soviet troops on the roads west from Budapest. At Komárom on the Danube, there was fierce fighting between a force made up of Hungarian soldiers and insurgents with Soviet troops attacking from both Hungarian territory and Czechoslovakia on the other side of the river. In the major planned industrial town of Dunapentele, formerly known as Sztálinváros, there was also fierce fighting as a force made up of workers from the factories along with officers and soldiers from the local Hungarian army garrison faced an attack by Soviet armour, including tanks and self-propelled guns, supported by air strikes.

The UN investigation later noted that 'the Committee cannot but conclude that the Hungarian resistance to the second Soviet intervention was a heroic demonstration of the will of the Hungarian people to fight for their national independence'.

And what of the man who had become the leader of independent Hungary? Once the Soviet attack had been launched, Imre Nagy left the Parliament building. He may have intended to go to the Soviet embassy to protest to Andropov but if so he presumably had second thoughts about such a rash course of action; instead he arrived at the Yugoslav embassy at about 6 a.m., where he formally requested asylum. (In the early hours of the morning, the Yugoslavs had offered Nagy asylum through a Hungarian intermediary and Nagy had accepted this lifeline.) Although much of the Brioni deal between Tito and Khrushchev remains obscure, part of it was an agreement by the Yugoslavs to keep Nagy out of the way while the Soviet military dealt with the insurgents. Throughout the remainder of November, the government of Yugoslavia negotiated with the Kádár regime over the terms on which Nagy and other Hungarians who were sheltering in the Yugoslav embassy might safely leave. Kádár informed the Yugoslav ambassador that he wanted Nagy and the others with him to seek asylum in Romania until the situation in Hungary had calmed down; Nagy and his group declared that they preferred to stay in Hungary if offered written guarantees of their safety or to seek asylum in Yugoslavia. However, Tito was not prepared to run the risk of offending Moscow by accepting Nagy. On 22 November, the Yugoslavs informed Kádár that they would only agree to the departure of Nagy and the others if Kádár would provide a written guarantee of safe conduct to their homes. Kádár responded that his government had no desire to punish Nagy and the others. Although Nagy did not trust Kádár, he thought the new government was still too weak politically to break a written promise and assumed that the Soviets had no desire to harm him. The next day, a bus arrived at the embassy to take the group of Hungarians home; when Soviet troops arrived and insisted on boarding the bus, the Yugoslav ambassador asked that two of his officials should go with the group to make sure that they arrived home. The bus then drove to Soviet military headquarters, where the two Yugoslav officials were ordered to leave by a Russian lieutenant-colonel. Accompanied by two Soviet armoured vehicles, the bus drove away. Outraged, the Yugoslav government announced this to be 'a flagrant breach of the agreement reached' and condemned what had happened as completely contrary to international law. The plan had been Andropov's, enthusiastically approved by Serov, and despite their protest it seems that the Yugoslavs had known in advance what was going to happen.

Nagy was taken to Romania and held there in Snagov castle near Bucharest until 1958, when he was returned to Hungary to be tried in secret on charges of treason and organizing the overthrowing of the Hungarian people's democratic state. Found guilty and sentenced to death, Nagy was hanged in June 1958 and buried in an unmarked grave, as was the former minister of defence, Pál Maléter. It has long been assumed that it was the Soviets who were responsible for the death of Imre Nagy. However, documents are now available that suggest that Kádár may have been keener to execute Nagy than Moscow was; Kádár had concluded that his predecessor, even in prison, would always be a rival and wanted to be rid of him once and for all. Khrushchev's son has said that although his father defended Nagy's arrest, he was rather less happy about his execution.

On 7 November, while the Soviets were celebrating the anniversary of the Russian Revolution, Kádár finally arrived back in Budapest. Although he was the prime minister, real authority in the city rested with the Soviets, with Serov and with Grebenyik, the military commander. Although active resistance to the Soviets had ended, the resentful population mounted a campaign of passive resistance and a general strike. Kádár tried to negotiate an end to the strike with Sándor Rácz of the Central Workers' Council of Greater Budapest. They agreed to lift the strikes to allow the delivery of food and to ensure that heating could be provided but quarrelled over the status of the Central Workers' Council, after which Kádár decided that he would need to deal with the revolutionary workers' councils. For the time being, he continued with his policy of conciliation. Part of his strategy was to complain about the harder line that the Soviets were taking and the tactics that they were using to enforce that line, as well as their habit of countermanding his agreements and reaching decisions without informing him. However, Kádár's conciliation only went so far and eventually he cracked down.

Above and below: Women march silently through the streets of Budapest in December 1956 to mourn the crushing of the uprising. (Fortepan: Nagy Gyula)

A notice calling for a strike to show opposition to the Soviets. (Fortepan: Pesti Srác 2)

Kádár set up a new security service, the Karhatalom, which many former members of the AVH joined. The Karhatalom's R Section was specifically responsible for reprisals against those involved in the uprising and although they did not carry out an indiscriminate purge as many Hungarians feared, they were extremely efficient in tracking down their prey. In all, it is thought that as many as 500 people may have been executed for their parts in the Hungarian Uprising, although fewer than half that number of death sentences were officially passed, and that the executions may have continued until 1960 as before that some of those condemned would have been under the statutory age of eighteen. Others died in prison; Nagy's friend Geza Losonczy had died in December 1957 from injuries inflicted on him during force-feeding after he had gone on hunger strike. Although Losonczy was officially said to have died of illness, he was heard by another prisoner shouting, 'Help me! They are killing me!'

Above is a suggestion that Kádár should be hanged, while below is a more general appeal for 'loyal Hungarians' to oppose him. (Fortepan: Budapest Főváros Levéltára)

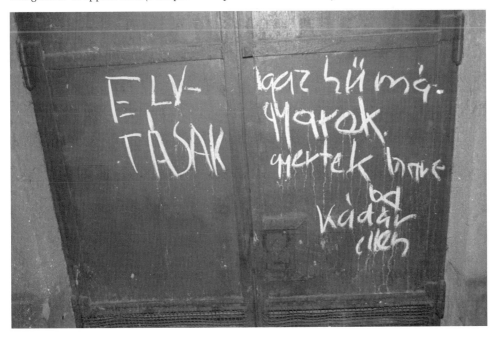

The Russians too were carrying out arrests and hundreds of Hungarians were deported to the Soviet Union. However, the deportations soon stopped and those deported were sent back to Hungary as it had been decided that they could just as easily be dealt with there.

After the crackdown, Kádár allowed a thaw to set in. From spring 1957, Soviet soldiers stationed near Budapest were confined to their barracks and those farther away from the capital kept a low profile and tried to attract less attention – their officers, for example, would wear civilian clothes when they went out. Over the next three years, Soviet forces in Hungary would halve in number. Meanwhile, huge loans from the Soviet government meant that wages increased by some 15 to 20 per cent from the summer of 1957. Kádár tried to show that his government was not as completely subservient to Moscow as those of Rákosi and Gerő had been. There were amnesties for some of those involved in the uprising, and then a final, full amnesty in 1962. However, there was an almost complete silence over the events of 1956 and Nagy's name was not mentioned in public. Loathing publicity, Kádár further distinguished himself from his predecessors by discouraging a cult of personality. He would always maintain that if he had not agreed to take power in November 1956, someone worse would have been brought in and Hungarians accepted this and gave him credit for making Hungary the most prosperous and easygoing of the Soviet bloc without forgetting the circumstances in which he had come to power.

Kádár ruled Hungary from November 1956 until his removal from office by younger, more reform-minded figures in the Party in 1988. He died the following year, at the age of seventy-seven. Kádár had outlived both Mátyás Rákosi and Ernő Gerő. Rákosi, having been forced to move to the Soviet Union in 1956, spent the rest of his life in what is now Kyrgyzstan in Central Asia. In 1970 Rákosi was allowed to move back to Hungary on condition that he promised not to engage in politics; he declined the offer and died the following year in the Soviet city of Gorky, now Nizhny Novgorod on the Volga. Gerő was permitted to return from his exile in the Soviet Union in 1960 but was expelled in short order from the Communist Party to ensure that he could not cause trouble for Kádár. He lived in Budapest for the next twenty years and worked occasionally as a translator.

Cardinal Mindszenty had been granted asylum at the US legation and would end up spending the next fifteen years there, at considerable inconvenience to his hosts, unable to leave the grounds for fear of being re-arrested. In the late 1960s, Mindszenty's health began to decline and there were rumours that he was dying

János Kádár with members of the Young Pioneers, the communist youth movement, in 1973. (Fortepan: Urbán Tamás)

János Kádár at May Day celebrations in 1962. (Fortepan: Magyar Rendőr)

but Kádár was reluctant to agree to let him leave. A deal was eventually brokered by Pope Paul VI and the Hungarian government allowed the cardinal to leave the country on 28 September 1971. Mindszenty would die in Vienna in May 1975, at the age of eighty-three.

In January 1989 a member of the Hungarian politburo, Rezsö Nyers, offered his opinion that the uprising had been a 'people's uprising' rather than a counter-revolution and said: 'Imre Nagy was not a counter-revolutionary, he was not ... Where the hell do we find counter-revolutionary ideas with Imre Nagy? Nowhere, absolutely nowhere!' Nyers was commenting on the report issued by a historical committee that had been set up by the Hungarian government to re-examine the events of 1956. Once the Soviet government, now led by the reformist Mikhail Gorbachev, indicated that it did not object, the Hungarians organized a reburial for Imre Nagy's remains. The movement in Hungary to rehabilitate Imre Nagy did not go un-noticed or un-challenged. In the Soviet Union, KGB Chairman Vladimir Kryuchkov reported that the KGB archives indicated that when Nagy had been in Moscow in the 1930s, he 'sought out contact with the security organs [i.e. the secret police] and in 1933 volunteered to become an agent (a secret informer)'. Nagy had apparently been enthusiastic about his work and his evidence had led to several arrests and some executions. Kryuchkov suggested that this information be passed on to the Hungarians to counter the campaign to rehabilitate Nagy. A hardliner, Kryuchkov would later be involved in the plot to overthrow Mikhail Gorbachev that led to the collapse of the Soviet Union. Kryuchkov's revelations apparently did little to change minds. When Nagy was reburied in Budapest on 16 June 1989, some 200,000 people lined the streets to watch.

5. INTERNATIONAL REACTION AND AFTERMATH

When looking to offer a public or official explanation for what had happened in Hungary, the Soviet government reached for Marxist dialectic. In Marxist theory, there is a concept of 'historical inevitability' – i.e. it is inevitable that societies will eventually move to embrace communism because any other form of government is profoundly unfair towards the workers despite the fact that 'crimes' and 'mistakes' could happen in a communist society. It is therefore impossible, contrary to the predestined course of history, that once a communist system has been put in place, the population should find sufficient fault with it to reject it and return to the system in place before. If radical criticism of the system is offered, this cannot be because of a desire to improve things; it must be a bourgeois trick to mislead the workers and reintroduce a capitalist system that will exploit them. The official Soviet line was that the Hungarian Uprising was just such a bourgeois trick intended to allow the re-introduction of capitalism. On 18 December 1956, an edition of *Pravda* – the official newspaper of the Soviet Communist Party – was devoted to Hungary and its editorial stated: 'So long as there are exploiters and exploited in the world, so long as there are capitalists holding power in their hands and the working class, so long will the conflict between the bourgeoisie and the proletariat remain the starting point for an analysis of historical events. Revisionism has repeatedly attempted to snatch from the hands of the working class this Marxist compass, which enables one to give a correct appraisal of the direction of events.' The new regime in Hungary echoed that line. The Hungarian mission at the UN described the aim of the uprising as being 'to reinstate the system of capitalists and estate owners, who have never given up hope since their defeat in 1945'. Although the Hungarian population may have had legitimate grievances against the Rákosi and Gerő governments, these were exploited by Hungarian émigrés and foreign governments looking to overthrow the communist system in Hungary.

Regardless of the theoretical interpretation placed on it by Moscow, the real message of the Hungarian Uprising was not lost on those watching from elsewhere in the Soviet bloc: the USSR would not tolerate any signs of rebellion. The result was that there was barely any sign of opposition to Soviet control in Eastern Europe for more than ten years. However, the speed with which the one-party state in Hungary had collapsed had come as a nasty surprise to Khrushchev and those around him in the Kremlin and as a result they developed something of a 'Hungary complex'.

Outside the Soviet bloc, the suppression of Hungary also had its effect. The Chinese embassy in Budapest reported back to Beijing that the communist authorities had had trouble ensuring that everyone toed the line ideologically: 'A good number of comrades did not clearly see the Hungarian way of think-ing and frame of mind, but after thorough criticism they showed great improve-ment, even if they have not yet defeated [their incorrect views].' A Soviet Foreign Ministry assessment of the combined fallout from Hungary and the Suez Crisis suggested that in some Third World countries, 'an analogy was made between the English-French-Israeli aggression in Egypt and the participation of Soviet forces in the suppression of the counter-revolutionary revolt in Hungary'. It also noted that 'Recent events in Hungary and in the Near East and the position of the USA during these events have made possible an increase in the prestige of the USA in Asian countries.'

The communist parties in Western Europe also did not find it easy to hold to the official line and suffered from fractures between those who supported it and those who did not. The French and Italian communist parties had been especially strong but this changed after Hungary. In the French Communist Party, moder-ate members such as philosopher Jean-Paul Sartre and the historian Emmanuel Le Roy Ladurie criticized the Soviet response to the Hungarian Uprising and questioned the party's support for Moscow. Italian Communist leader Palmiro Togliatti reported to Moscow that 'Hungarian events have developed in a way that render our clarifying action in the Party very difficult' and added that 'it also makes it difficult to obtain consensus in favour of the leadership'. Many major figures in the Italian Communist Party would repudiate the party line on events in Hungary and either left or were expelled from the party as a result. In Britain the Communist Party of Great Britain (CPGB) had begun to fracture as a result of Khrushchev's Secret Speech and the events that had followed and Hungary only speeded this up: it was estimated that somewhere between a quarter and a third of party members left as a result of the events of 1956. Peter Fryer, a corre-spondent for the CPGB newspaper the *Daily Worker*, was an eyewitness to events in Hungary and covered what happened for the newspaper but his reports were either censored or never appeared; he would later be expelled from the CPGB for criticizing the suppression of the Hungarian Uprising. Fryer would specifically state: 'This was no counter-revolution ... It was the upsurge of a whole people, in which rank and file communists took part, against a police dictatorship dressed up as a Socialist society.' The Danish Communist Party simply disappeared entirely.

Beyond the communist parties, the reaction in the West was outrage but not much more than that. The problem for the United States was that events in the Middle East made it difficult for the US to criticize what the Soviet Union was doing in Hungary. On 31 October, Britain and France had started Operation Musketeer, a plan to seize the Suez Canal (which had been nationalized by the Egyptian government, led by Gamal Abdel Nasser, on 26 July) by force and occupy it in order to preserve Western control of the canal. British and French troops were landed in Egypt and bombing raids and air strikes launched. Despite admitting in a letter to Prime Minister Anthony Eden that Britain had legitimate interests in Egypt, Soviet Premier Nikolai Bulganin threatened Soviet intervention in

Corpses in Köztársaság Square, Budapest. (Photo Fortepan: Pesti Srác)

favour of Egypt; this would include nuclear missile attacks on Britain, France and Israel (whose attack on Egypt, coordinated with Britain and France, was the pretext for Anglo-French intervention). After the ending of the Suez Crisis, Nasser publicly thanked Khrushchev for saving Egypt; it was widely believed that it was the Soviet threats of nuclear war that forced a ceasefire and Anglo-French withdrawal from Suez. Soviet prestige in the Middle East and elsewhere rose accordingly. In June 1957, Mikoyan said that after the Hungarian Uprising and the Soviet confrontation with Poland over Gomułka, the Soviets had lost prestige. He suggested that the timing of the Anglo-French invasion had been intended to take advantage of the Soviet preoccupation with Hungary but that 'we found both the strength to keep troops in Hungary and to threaten the imperialists that if they do not end the war in Egypt, it could lead to the use of missile weapons by us'. One interpretation of the effect of the Suez Crisis on the Western response to Hungary was that the Western powers were unwilling to provoke the Soviets and risk nuclear war: if Moscow was willing to threaten nuclear war over Suez, how would they react to intervention in the Soviet bloc in Eastern Europe?

Although Eisenhower certainly worried that the Suez Crisis might be the start of a third world war involving nuclear weapons, the US began to investigate whether the Soviets really possessed the nuclear arsenal that Khrushchev claimed that they did and by early 1959 it was clear that they did not and that Khrushchev had been heavily exaggerating. Indeed, it turned out that Nasser too had been exaggerating when he hailed the effect of Soviet threats in making Britain and France back down: he later acknowledged that it had been American financial pressure that had actually saved Egypt. The American response to the Anglo-French invasion of Suez was to apply financial pressure to Britain: the Americans threatened to cause a run on the pound by selling part of their holdings of UK bonds. Devaluing sterling would have wiped out Britain's foreign exchange reserves and meant that the country would soon be unable to import the food and oil supplies that it needed. The US also supported an oil embargo imposed on Britain and France by Saudi Arabia and other Arab nations.

President Eisenhower had decided that Egypt was more important to the US than Hungary was. When reports had arrived in Washington that the communist government in Hungary was collapsing, Eisenhower had immediately decided not to intervene. He did not believe that the American public would support a war with the Soviets over Hungary and was anxious not to give Moscow an excuse to accuse the US of meddling. Eisenhower also did not want to be distracted by events in Eastern Europe as the Suez Crisis was starting to come to a head: he felt that the US would be more able to make a difference in the Middle East than in Eastern Europe where the status quo was more fixed and where trying to change it would come with more risks. He was concerned about the possibility that the Arab world might become pro-Soviet if the United States was perceived to have acquiesced in the Suez invasion. As Nixon pointed out, it was politically impossible for the United States to complain about Soviet intervention in Hungary and at the same time approve of the Anglo-French intervention in Egypt. (A similar point was made in Britain that the Suez invasion made it impossible for the British government to oppose Soviet intervention in Hungary, for example in a letter written by Lady Violet Bonham Carter to *The Times*)

Rendered unable to act by the situation in Egypt, the US attempted to respond to the Hungarian Uprising covertly, using the CIA and Radio Free Europe. However, the CIA's ignorance of the situation in Hungary in the run-up to the uprising and the effectiveness of the AVH in dealing with covert CIA agents and the arms caches that the Americans had attempted to conceal in Hungary meant that the agency was largely ineffective. Radio Free Europe maintained a pugnacious stream of programming that offered advice (including, for example, ways of fighting against tanks) and encouragement to the insurgents. The role of Radio Free Europe in the uprising was controversial at the time and remains so now, the chief question being whether the station prolonged the fighting by leading Hungarians to believe that if they continued to resist, NATO or the UN would intervene. The Kádár government certainly professed to believe in the importance of RFE to the uprising, describing its 'subversive broadcasts' as having 'played an essential role in the ideological preparation and practical direction of the counter-revolution'. The UN noted that 'Listeners had the feeling that Radio Free Europe promised help, although witnesses said clearly that it gave no reason for expecting military help. Rather, the general tone of these broadcasts aroused an expectation of support'. The West German Chancellor, Konrad Adenauer, went somewhat further and said that 'remarks were also made which were liable to cause misinterpretations'. The CIA launched its own internal investigation into the role that RFE had played in the uprising and concluded that there had been times when the station had crossed the line and broken CIA guidelines in what it had broadcast, offering tactical advice to the revolutionaries, but that these had not been deliberate. Radio Free Europe, the CIA concluded, had not provoked the uprising.

A poster dating from 1958 commemorating a propaganda tour to the Philippines undertaken by veterans of the uprising to promote opposition to communism. (US National Archives)

Nevertheless, events in Hungary had proved damaging to the credibility of both the United States and President Eisenhower personally. The uprising had exposed the gap between Washington's rhetoric about rolling back communism and liberating the captive peoples of Eastern Europe and what the United States was prepared to do as a matter of practical policy to help achieve that. Eisenhower was very sensitive to criticism of this sort and defended himself in an interview with *The New York Times* on 14 November 1956. He told the paper that 'The US does not now and never has advocated open rebellion by an undefended populace against force over which it could not possibly prevail.' The president then went on to say that 'we have never, in all the years that I think we have been dealing with problems of this sort, urged or argued for any kind of armed revolt which could bring about disaster to our friends'.

In response to resolutions in the UN General Assembly requesting investigation and observation of events in Hungary, Secretary-General Dag Hammarskjöld set up the Special Committee on the Problem of Hungary. Chaired by Alsing Andersen of Denmark and containing representatives from Australia, Ceylon, Tunisia and Uruguay, the committee was asked to provide the General Assembly with 'the fullest and best available information regarding the situation created by the intervention of the [USSR] ... in the internal affairs of Hungary'. In the course of its investigation, the committee interviewed 111 witnesses in New York, Geneva, Rome, Vienna and London. Hungary and Romania refused to allow officials from the committee to enter either country and the Soviet government made no response to requests for information. The committee's 268-page final report, issued in June 1957, concluded that the uprising had been spontaneous, that 'the few days of freedom enjoyed by the Hungarian people provided abundant evidence of the popular nature of the uprising' and that if there had been any counter-revolution in Hungary it was the imposition using armed Soviet troops of the Kádár government in place of that of Imre Nagy, which had enjoyed overwhelming popular support.

There was little else that the United Nations could realistically have done, even if the organization had not already decided to focus on the Suez Crisis. The Soviets possessed a veto in the Security Council and also had the advantage of force majeure on the ground while the US was concentrating on Suez. Hammarskjöld would later be asked why he had not gone to Budapest at the start of November, when he might still have been able to negotiate with the Soviets. His response was that although the Security Council knew nothing at the time about what was happening in Budapest, they did know what was happening in Egypt. And so the UN concentrated its attention on what was happening in Egypt.

The refusal of Hungary, Romania and the Soviet Union to cooperate with the UN report on the Hungarian Uprising did not go un-noticed. In a conversation with China's foreign minister, Zhou Enlai, Prime Minister Nehru of India said that he thought that 'this type of action could easily cause Hungary to lose the sympathy of the majority of United Nations countries'. He also observed that 'the

Soviets' dispatch of troops, and especially sending Nagy to Romania after he left the Yugoslav embassy, put the Soviet Union in an extremely disadvantageous and passive position in the face of world opinion'. However, when Zhou suggested that Western countries had taken advantage of the situation to carry out 'subversive activities' in Hungary, Nehru agreed and also said that it would have been very dangerous for Hungary to have left the Soviet bloc.

One of the major consequences of the Hungarian Uprising outside of Hungary itself was the major outflow of refugees. As of 11 March 1957, the UNHCR estimated that nearly 200,000 Hungarians had fled the country; roughly 20,000 had crossed Hungary's southern border into Yugoslavia and the others had crossed the western border into Austria. A report for NATO estimated that before the uprising, an average of sixty-six Hungarians had crossed the border into Austria every month. In November, as the Soviets cracked down, this increased to the point where 46,000 refugees crossed the border in one week. Even in the first half of January 1957, as many as 800 refugees arrived, although by March that figure had gone down to ten or fifteen a day. It seems that through November and into the first week of December Kádár and the Soviets had not worried too much about people escaping from the country, perhaps hoping that given the opportunity most of the potential troublemakers in the country would leave of their own accord. Large parts of the Austrian border were left unguarded by Soviet troops with the result that once refugees reached the border, they could simply walk out of the country.

The refugees were described as being made up of 'a high proportion of male industrial workers between the ages of 16 and 40, with a spearhead of students and intellectuals ... and a leavening of members of the former middle classes'. Some of these had been prominent figures in the uprising and were fleeing death sentences while others would have risked long prison sentences if they had stayed in Hungary. Of the rest, many feared that the Soviets would seek revenge in the form of a campaign of terror like that launched by Rákosi after the Rajk trial. As the refugees were generally keen to move on from Austria and Yugoslavia, the problems were getting sufficient offers of resettlement and finding the money to pay for everything. Eventually, the United States accepted some 150,000 Hungarian refugees and Britain and France each accepted nearly 30,000.

Covering the reburial of Imre Nagy in 1989, *The New York Times* asked the question 'Can the Past be Re-buried?' The *Times* article described how 'Hungary's greatest political taboo has become a favorite topic for the press and broadcasters':

Hungarian refugees at a Red Cross kitchen in Austria. (Photo ICRC)

surviving veterans of the uprising and the widows and children of those who had died, long condemned to deliberate obscurity by the authorities, were now appearing regularly in the Hungarian media and questions that once would have been unthinkable were now being asked in public. The Writers' Union weekly, *Elet es Irodalom* (Life and Literature), for example, published an article asking questions about János Kádár and his role during the end of the uprising and calling on him to explain himself. The former prime minister, however, died a month after his predecessor was reburied.

It is difficult to know for certain why Kádár made the decision that he did in November 1956. It seems unlikely that a refusal by Kádár to cooperate with the Soviets would have made a great deal of difference in how the uprising ended – the Kremlin magnates had already decided to forcibly end the uprising, and who would take power in Budapest after Nagy was deposed was a separate question. The key point to remember is that the majority of the decisions that changed how events would play out in Budapest during late October and early November 1956 were taken in Moscow. It was the Kremlin that decided to approve the intervention of Soviet troops at the start of the uprising, it was the Kremlin that approved the ceasefire and the declaration that promised a new relationship between the USSR and the satellite states and in the end it was the Kremlin that decided that a red line had been crossed and to forcibly suppress the uprising.

The key decisions taken in Washington were not to intervene in Hungary and to focus on the crisis in the Middle East. American influence in the events of 1956 is significant by its absence, despite the enduring question of whether US propaganda helped to fan the flames. If it did, the fire had already been lit by the behaviour of the Rákosi and Gerő governments and by the pervasive Soviet influence that seemed so offensive to so many in Hungary.

Nagy's reburial would later prove to have been a landmark moment in the end of communism in Hungary later that year and a sign that at least as far as 1956 was concerned, the past was not as easy to rebury as the authorities may have hoped. Indeed, the date on which communist Hungary ceased to be and the new democratic, free-market Hungary took its place in 1989 was 23 October.

With little fuss, Stalin's statue comes down, 23 October 1956. (Fortepan: Pesti srác2)